The Yachtsman's Pilot to the West Coast of Scotland
Clyde to Colonsay

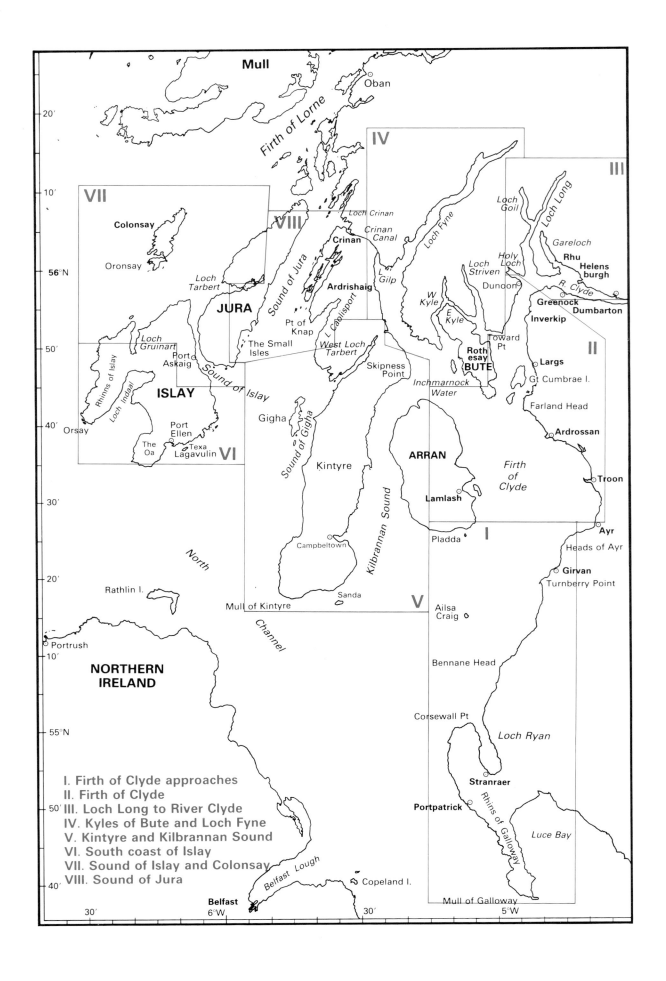

Mull

Oban

Firth of Lorne

IV

III

Loch Crinan

Crinan Canal

Loch Goil

Loch Long

Gareloch

VII

Colonsay

VIII

Loch Fyne

Rhu

Helens burgh

Oronsay

Crinan

Loch Tarbert

Ardrishaig

L. Gilp

Loch Striven

Holy Loch

R. Clyde

Dunoon

Greenock

Dumbarton

JURA

Sound of Jura

Pt of Knap

L Caolisport

W Kyle

E Kyle

Toward Pt

Inverkip

II

Loch Gruinart

The Small Isles

West Loch Tarbert

Roth esay

BUTE

Largs

Port Askaig

Skipness Point

Gt Cumbrae I.

ISLAY

Sound of Islay

Inchmarnock Water

Farland Head

Rhinns of Islay

Loch Indaal

Gigha

Sound of Gigha

ARRAN

Firth of Clyde

Ardrossan

Orsay

Port Ellen

The Oa

Texa

Lagavulin

VI

Kintyre

Kilbrannan Sound

Lamlash

Troon

Ayr

Pladda

I

Heads of Ayr

Girvan

Turnberry Point

North

Rathlin I.

Campbeltown

Sanda

V

Ailsa Craig

Bennane Head

NORTHERN IRELAND

Channel

Mull of Kintyre

Corsewall Pt

Loch Ryan

Portrush

Stranraer

I. Firth of Clyde approaches
II. Firth of Clyde
III. Loch Long to River Clyde
IV. Kyles of Bute and Loch Fyne
V. Kintyre and Kilbrannan Sound
VI. South coast of Islay
VII. Sound of Islay and Colonsay
VIII. Sound of Jura

Portpatrick

Rhins of Galloway

Luce Bay

Belfast Lough

Copeland I.

Belfast

Mull of Galloway

20'

10'

56°N

50'

40'

30'

20'

10'

55°N

50'

40'

30'

6°W

30'

5°W

The Yachtsman's Pilot to the West Coast of Scotland
Clyde to Colonsay

MARTIN LAWRENCE

Imray Laurie Norie & Wilson Ltd
St Ives Cambridgeshire England

Published by
Imray, Laurie, Norie & Wilson Ltd
Wych House, St Ives, Huntingdon,
Cambridgeshire, PE17 4BT, England.

© Martin Lawrence 1989

British Library Cataloguing in Publication Data

Lawrence, Martin, 1939–
   Clyde to Colonsay.
   1. Western Scotland. Coastal waters – Pilots' guides
   I. Title   II. Series
   623.89'29411

   ISBN 0 85288 132 0

CAUTION
Whilst every care has been taken to ensure accuracy, neither the Publishers nor the Author will hold themselves responsible for errors, omissions or alterations in this publication. They will at all times be grateful to receive information which tends to the improvement of the work.

PLANS
The plans in this guide are not to be used for navigation. They are designed to support the text and should at all times be used with navigational charts.

The last input of technical information was June 1989.

Set in Plantin by Cromwell Graphics Ltd, St Ives, Huntingdon direct from the Author's and Publishers' disks.

Printed at The Bath Press, Avon

Contents

Preface and acknowledgements, vi

Introduction, 1
  Travel, 2
  Passage making, 2
  Submarines, 3
  Tides, 3
  Weather, 3
  Anchorages, 3
  Communications, 6
  Emergencies, 7
  Notes on plans and pilotage directions, 7

    I. Firth of Clyde approaches, 9
   II. Firth of Clyde, 21
  III. Loch Long to River Clyde, 43
  IV. Kyles of Bute and Loch Fyne, 57
   V. Kintyre and Kilbrannan Sound, 83
  VI. South coast of Islay, 103
 VII. Sound of Islay and Colonsay, 119
VIII. Sound of Jura, 131

Appendix
    I. Charts and other publications, 145
   II. Glossary of Gaelic words, 148
  III. Quick reference table of provisions, services
       and supplies, 149
  IV. Conversion tables, 150

Index, 151

Preface

Sailing directions published for other cruising areas have for many years been well illustrated with photographs or drawings. Views from seaward, both of transits and for identification, used to be a feature of Admiralty charts and pilots; no doubt with electronic aids they were thought unnecessary, but their usefulness is being rediscovered and some Admiralty pilots now incorporate views originally drawn for yachtsmen's pilots.

The photos in this book were taken mainly at low spring tides to reveal as many hazards as possible. However if coverage isn't as comprehensive, and some of the photos not as clear as might be, this is because it takes many years to visit each place at a specific time of day and month, whether by sea, land or air – with no guarantee that conditions will be suitable for photography when one gets there.

Inevitably a book of this kind is flavoured by the author's outlook and experience, and it may be helpful to know that for ten years I have owned a steel ketch of traditional character and perhaps take a slightly more light-hearted view of rock-dodging than the owner of a less robust vessel would do. On the other hand *Erraid* is not so handy as most GRP cruiser-racers, and any place into which she can find her way should present little difficulty to a modern yacht of moderate size.

In addition to current Admiralty charts, older charts often include additional information about tidal streams, etc. I have also been able to refer to original Admiralty surveys, many of them made about 1860 in meticulous detail and drawn at a much larger scale than published charts. Aerial survey photos particularly by the RAF reveal a wealth of detail when they are taken under suitable light conditions.

Published accounts of cruises supply occasional clues, and individual yachtsmen provide information including, occasionally, sketch plans. Sometimes, however this information is conflicting and a choice has to be made between them. I once received three plans of Glas Uig in Islay, all different and all from reliable sources; fortunately by then I knew the place a bit better myself and was able to select between them.

Even where the information seems adequate it has to be compared with other sources and checked for new developments (and rumours of developments).

These directions can be no more than the sum of my own and other people's observations together with a summary of all that I have read, and gleaned from charts and air photos, and various published sources. There could well be hazards which I have missed by luck rather than good management and in spite of all the efforts of Imray's editorial team there may be simple errors which have been overlooked; even supplements to Admiralty pilots contain the occasional instruction 'for E read W'.

The directions should be compared with charts and all other information available before an approach is made, to ensure that they are understood and correspond. If you find directions which you think are inaccurate, or changes which have occurred since the publication of this volume, I should be very grateful if you would let me know, through the Publishers.

Anyone who sails regularly on the Clyde and west coast of Scotland should apply to join the Clyde Cruising Club; the club is active on behalf of yachtsmen throughout the area and arranges a stimulating programme of racing and cruising events. The club's address is: S.V. Carrick, Clyde Street, Glasgow G1 4LN, ☎ 041-552 2183.

Acknowledgements

The initiative for this pilot came from Nigel Gardner, who also provided much detailed information. Information was also provided by: Doris Bohndorf, of Scottish German Charters; Michael Gilkes, whose knowledge of the southeast coast of Islay is unequalled; D. Glover, of Portnahaven, Islay; George Jarvis, who has probably landed on every rock in the Sound of Jura that ever shows its head above water; R. W. Macleman of Ayr Yacht and Cruising Club; Bruce Montgomery-Smith, Montgomery-Smith and Partners, engineers for the HIDB facilities for visiting yachts; D. Skinner, Commodore of Loch Ryan Sailing Club; John Stewart of Campbeltown Sailing Club (and second coxswain of Campbeltown lifeboat); Ian Wallace of Borroboats, Oban; and Laurence Wilson, secretary to the Girvan lifeboat.

The production of the book itself owes an enormous amount to the work put in by various people: the text was made more readable by my wife's efforts to disentangle it; further order was introduced by Imray's editor, Nell Stuart, who also meticulously checked every detail. The final form of the plans is due to the work of Imray's cartographers, to whom I gave only the outlines and rough notes. Some of the drawings of transits are by Harriet Lawrence.

The Publishers are grateful to Elizabeth Cook who compiled the index.

Martin Lawrence
Edinburgh
May 1989

Most of the plans in this book are based on British Admiralty charts with the permission of the Hydrographer of the Navy and the sanction of H. M. Stationery Office.

Introduction

The series of pilots of which this is one part sets out to provide useful information for visitors to the Firth of Clyde and west coast of Scotland in pleasure boats as clearly as possible. It is not trying to 'sell' the West Coast; anyone reading it is probably already considering sailing there. The upper limit of size for which it caters is a draught of 2 metres, but there is information specifically for shoal-draught boats – centreboarders, trailer-sailers, twin-keel boats and multihulls, and of course motor-cruisers, who tend to be forgotten by writers of 'sailing directions' who usually seem to own sailing boats.

The Clyde and west coast of Scotland have traditionally been regarded as deep-water areas, but there are many anchorages or parts of anchorages only accessible to shoal-draught boats, particularly those which can dry out fairly upright. In most other areas, having a shoal-draught boat is the best way to avoid the crowds, and this is increasingly becoming the case on the west coast of Scotland.

For trailer-sailers the easiest place on the Clyde to launch a boat trailed from a distance is Barrfield Slip at Largs. However it is moderately exposed, and marinas may have a slip available for a charge.

The smallest boats, even dinghies, may be able to cruise in much of the area described in this pilot, but they must be soundly equipped and competently handled by experienced crews. Except within some very sheltered lochs, the Clyde and west coast of Scotland are not suitable for those who are unable to deal with adverse conditions which may arise unexpectedly.

Much of the area covered by this volume is sheltered by islands or within lochs which penetrate far among some of the highest hills in Britain. This shelter creates problems of its own, particularly the squalls which are generated in the lee of hills, as well as the higher rainfall.

Anyone who is capable of managing a yacht at a comparable distance from the shore whether in the North Sea, the Baltic, the English Channel, the Atlantic coast of France or the Irish Sea will have little problem on the west coast of Scotland.

Outwith the main channels of the Firth of Clyde there is little traffic, although a good lookout needs to be kept for fishing boats, and naval vessels (especially submarines) on exercises.

Visibility is usually good, except in rain: fog as such is fairly rare. The climate is wetter and cooler than, for example, the south coast of England (although the further west you go, away from the mainland hills, the drier the weather. A compensating factor is the longer daylight in summer, so that you rarely need to sail at night.

One of the main attractions of the West Coast is the sheer variety of anchorages and passages which occur within quite a small area. The directions in this book are divided into eight chapters, each covering waters of quite different character, from the industrial (and post-industrial) surroundings of the upper parts of the Firth of Clyde to the absolute remoteness of the west of Jura.

Charts This pilot is not intended as a substitute for Admiralty charts. Although many of the plans are at a larger scale than the charts, and include more detail, they only cover small areas, and it is essential to have plenty of charts on board. A complete list of current charts is given in Appendix I.

Some obsolete charts show more detail than any current one, sometimes at a larger scale, but the soundings on them are in feet and fathoms; these are referred to where appropriate. They should of course only be used to supplement current charts, not as a substitute for them. Although many people blithely observe that 'rocks don't move', new ones are discovered (sometimes the hard way), buoys are moved, and new features are constructed ashore. The more charts you have (corrected, of course, up to date) the less anxious your pilotage will be.

Imray's charts C63 and C64, whose boundaries correspond closely with the scope of this pilot, are ideal overall charts of the area.

Sketch charts published by the Clyde Cruising Club will be found more convenient to use in a small boat but they show less detail than the Admiralty charts and are not corrected so frequently.

Maps Ordnance Survey maps at 1:50,000 or Bartholomew's at 1:100,000 are well worth taking along to make up for the lack of topographical detail on current charts. In places where the charts are at a small scale the Ordnance Survey maps actually provide useful navigational detail.

Equipment should be as robust and reliable as for a yacht going a similar distance offshore anywhere in the English Channel or the North Sea. You should have at least two anchors, of the sizes recommended by anchor manufacturers or independent reference books, rather than those supplied as standard by boat manufacturers which are often on the light side. Chain rather than rope will prevent a yacht roving around in gusts, but if you do use rope it will help to have a weight which can be let down to the seabed on a traveller. So many yachts are now kept in marinas and only sail to another marina or harbour that anchoring is no longer an everyday operation, but on the West Coast it is essential that the crew is thoroughly familiar with anchor handling. It is no use relying on visitors' moorings being available; where they do exist they are quite likely to be already occupied.

Chartering and instruction Plenty of boats are available, both for bareboat and skippered charters, and also instructional cruises. Many of the operators are members of the Association of Scottish Yacht Charterers, whose brochure can be obtained from the Scottish Tourist Board. Most operators, including some owners of individual yachts, also advertise in yachting magazines.

A good way to gain experience on the West Coast is to take a berth on one of the skippered charter yachts or instructional courses which are available. There are also shore-based instructional courses in dinghies; for any of these courses see the current edition of the publication *On the Water*, available free from the Scottish Tourist Board, 23 Ravelston Place, Edinburgh EH4 3EU, ☎ 031-332 2433.

Travel

Transport Public transport in the area is fairly comprehensive. Most places on the east side of the Clyde are served by rail, including Helensburgh, Garelochead and Arrochar at the head of Loch Long, but excluding any part of the coast between Ayr and Stranraer.

Most other parts of the mainland have a bus service, as do Arran, Bute and Islay.

All inhabited islands (except Inchmarnock, Little Cumbrae and Holy Island) have a regular car ferry service . The ferry to Colonsay runs from Oban.

Campbeltown and Islay have an air service from Glasgow.

Details of all public transport services (as well as local boat and car hirers) north and west of the Clyde and for the whole of the rest of the Highlands are included in a combined timetable with the title *Getting Around the Highlands and Islands*, published by FHG Publications in association with the Highlands and Islands Development Board annually at a price (in 1988) of £2·50 including postage. The timetable is available from FHG Publications, Seedhill, Paisley PA1 1JN, ☎ 041-887 0428.

There are good roads to most parts of the mainland, but those on the Cowal peninsula, between the Firth of Clyde and Loch Fyne, are not suitable for trailers.

Trailed boats can be launched at Largs which is convenient for roads from the south. Each of the marinas has a mobile hoist, suitable for launching boats delivered by road.

Passage making

Most passages covered by this volume are within sounds or lochs or along a shore entailing only short hops across open sea, so that navigation is, in the main, a matter of pilotage by eye and satisfying yourself that what you see corresponds to the chart. It is useful to pick out from the chart transits such as tangents of islands, or beacons in line with headlands to give you position lines from time to time. Check by compass bearings as well, starting from some unmistakable prominent object.

Traditional clearing marks for avoiding unmarked dangers, based on transits of natural features, are often much easier to use than compass bearings particularly where there are strong currents. Bearings are given in the text as a check on identification, and drawings and photographs provided where possible.

At night main channels are very well lit, but lights may be difficult to pick out against shore lights. Most other channels are just adequately lit; for a passage under power or with a fair wind. A few anchorages or passages are very well lit for local commercial users. During June and July there is little need to sail at night unless you are going further afield.

Marine radiobeacons

Name	Frequency	Identification	Range	Seq.	Position
Rhinns of Islay	294·2	RN	70M	4	55°40'·4N 6°30'·7W
Altacarry Head	294·2	AH	50M	3	55°18'·1N 6°10'·2W
Pladda	294·2	DA	30M	1	55°25'·5N 5°07'·1W

Aerobeacons

Name	Frequency	Identification	Range	Seq.	Position
Turnberry	355	TRN	25M	Cont	55°18'·8N 4°47'·0W
New Galloway	399	NGY	35M	Cont	55°10'·6N 4°10'·0W

Submarines

Certain areas are designated on charts (including Imray charts) as 'Submarine Exercise Areas' and a good lookout should be kept for submarines in these areas. In 1988 one yacht was damaged, and another sunk, in the North Channel by submarines running at periscope depth. A naval spokesman has suggested that yachts should make themselves more conspicuous, which seems to be a step towards shifting the liability for such incidents onto the yachts. Naval vessels on the surface may show the signal flags NE2 when submarines are exercising nearby.

Tides

Within the Firth of Clyde and to the west of Islay and Jura the range of tide is up to 4 metres. In the area covered by Chapters VI and VIII and in the sound of Gigha the range is less than 2 metres, but in several passages in that area, and around the Mull of Kintyre, tidal streams run at up to 8 knots. Tidal streams are strong wherever the movement of a large body of water is constricted by narrows, and there are often overfalls at the seaward end of narrow passages, particularly with wind against tide. Overfalls also occur off many headlands, and eddies are formed, usually down-tide of a promontory or islet or even a submerged reef, but sometimes in a bay up-tide of the obstruction. There are also usually overfalls wherever two tidal streams meet. These eddies and overfalls are so common that they are often not mentioned individually.

Tidal streams The flood tide generally runs north and west; but read the paragraphs on tides in the *Notes on plans and pilotage directions* below.

Weather

Inshore forecasts are broadcast by coastguards on VHF Ch 67 every four hours from the following local times:

Oban Coastguard from 0240
Clyde Coastguard from 0020
Belfast Coastguard from 0305

Anchorages

This heading covers not only natural anchorages but also moorings and berths alongside pontoons or quays. Many places are only suitable for a short daytime visit in settled conditions and the inclusion of an anchorage is no indication that it is suitable for all conditions. It is the skipper's responsibility to decide whether to use an anchorage at all, and for how long in light of conditions (at the time and predicted) and all the information available. Even the most apparently sheltered place will sometimes have the crew standing anchor watches throughout the night.

The description 'occasional anchorage' is intended to convey that the place described is only suitable for use under certain conditions; perhaps for a brief visit ashore during daylight, or in winds from certain directions to await a change of wind or tide. I prefer this description to 'temporary anchorage' which might imply that the anchorage is always (or only) suitable for a brief daylight visit. The absence of the description 'occasional' should not be taken as a recommendation that an anchorage may be used in any weather.

Some anchorages, and particularly piers and boat harbours, are only suitable for shoal-draught boats, and this should be obvious from the description; the inclusion of an anchorage does not imply that it is suitable for any vessel.

Within some anchorages there are often several suitable places to lie depending on conditions and it is not always practicable to describe them all, or to mark each one on the plans. In any case, an anchorage suitable for a shoal-draught boat 6 metres long may be inaccessible to a 15-metre yacht with a draught of 2 metres, and a berth which would give shelter for the larger yacht might be uncomfortably exposed for the smaller.

Steep high ground to windward is unlikely to provide good shelter; in fresh winds there may be turbulent gusts on its lee side, or the wind may be deflected to blow from a completely different direction. After a hot windless day there may be a strong katabatic wind down the slope, usually in the early morning; such conditions are by no means unknown in Scotland. A valley to windward will channel and accelerate any wind through it. Trees to windward will absorb a lot of wind and provide good shelter.

Rivers, burns and streams generally carry down debris, often leaving a shallow or drying bank of stones, sand or silt, over which the unwary may swing, frequently in the middle of the night.

Within any anchorage the quality of the bottom may vary greatly. Mud is common, (usually where there is little current) but its density may not be consistent and there are likely to be patches of rock, boulders and stones; also clay, which tends to break out suddenly. Sand is also common, but sometimes it is so hard that an anchor, particularly a light one, will not dig in. Weed of all kinds appears to be on the increase, but it does vary from year to year.

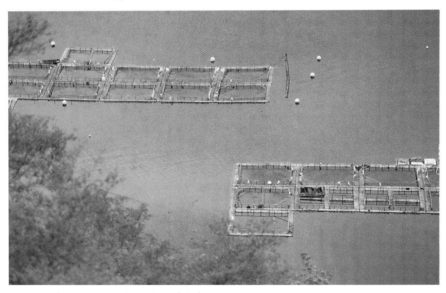

An increasingly common hazard – a fish farm.

Man-made obstructions Fishing floats, often insufficiently conspicuous, may be encountered even in very deep water, and a lookout has to be kept for them at all times but especially when motoring.

Fish farms are increasing at an alarming rate, usually outwith the most popular places, but attempts are sometimes made to establish them in recognised anchorages as well.

Permission to establish any permanent fixture on the seabed, such as a mooring, has to be obtained from the Crown Estates Commissioners who own the rights to the seabed; they consult the Department of Trade and Industry, who in turn consult RYA (Scotland), who consult whichever group of yachting interests may be appropriate, and they consult either the Clyde Cruising Club or the Royal Highland Yacht Club, one of whose more senior members will be asked for his comments; the comments are then passed back up the chain. The CEC are now much more aware of the needs of small craft.

Increasingly, moorings are being laid within established anchorages for fishing and other workboats as well as for yachts, and some traditional anchorages are now unusable by visiting boats. The West Highland Anchorages and Moorings Association, (WHAM), has been set up to concentrate on this problem; WHAM is at 8 Grianach Road, Oban.

Few yachtsmen whose moorings occupy cruising anchorages would object to their being used by visitors, but any visitor must be certain that the mooring is capable of holding his boat, must take reasonable steps to find out whether the owner is likely to return, and be ready to move if he does.

Visitors' moorings These may be seen as a convenience, necessity or obstruction depending on your point of view. Some are provided by local hotels free of charge to yachts whose crews patronise their establishments. They tend to be laid in the area most suitable for anchoring, and are arranged (as they have to be) to suit the largest boats likely to use them, and a boat on a mooring behaves differently from a boat at anchor. The effect is often to reduce the number of visiting boats which can use an anchorage. There is no guarantee that the mooring is suitable for any boat intending to use it.

HIDB moorings Visitors' moorings and pontoons have been provided by the Highlands and Islands Development Board in several places to bring more business to local traders, and the same comments apply to these moorings. The moorings have large blue buoys marked 'HIDB visitors' and '10 (or 15) tons'. There is no pick-up, and a rope has to be fed through a ring on top of the buoy. If your bow is so high that the buoy is out of reach and you cannot pass your rope through the ring, the best way to secure to one of these moorings is to lead a rope from the bow to the lowest point amidships, pick up the buoy there and take the end of the rope back to the bow.

Visiting yachts should raft up together on these moorings within the limits of the capacity of the mooring; no yacht can expect the exclusive use of an HIDB mooring if it has the capacity to hold another yacht.

Marinas have been established in the Firth of Clyde, and more are planned. A berth or mooring will usually be found for a visiting yacht, although the number of visitors sometimes exceeds the number of residents who are known to be away. If planning to leave a boat at as particular marina for a time, it should be arranged beforehand.

Commercial harbours Some harbours, mainly in the Firth of Clyde, are principally or entirely for commercial vessels, and yachts are either barely tolerated or not welcome; these should only be used in emergencies.

Piers and jetties, even in the most remote anchorages, are often privately owned or are treated as such by regular users, and should be treated in the same way as private moorings. Some are used by fishermen or workboats which may not treat an unattended yacht with as much delicacy as the owner would wish. Some piers are derelict and dangerous.

One solution to the moorings problem is to build your own harbour.

Upper Loch Long from south. Dog Rock is on the left, with
Finnart Oil Terminal beyond, to the right.

Eating ashore The prospect of eating and drinking ashore is a good deal less bleak than it was even ten years ago; hotels, restaurants and pubs are mentioned in the text, although not usually by name and without specific recommendations as management and standards may change rapidly.

Activities ashore For many yachtsmen (and their families) the places visited are as much part of a cruising holiday as the sailing. Some indoor entertainments are welcome if only as a refuge from bad weather, and museums are mentioned where applicable. There are castles and antiquities, birds and wildlife, and hills for walking.

Communications

Phone boxes are fairly well distributed and are referred to where known, but the 'rationalisation' of the telephone service may lead to a reduction in their numbers.

VHF radiotelephones The mountainous nature of this coast puts some areas out of range of either the coastguard or coast radio stations. Several yacht centres have VHF R/T, but they may not be continuously manned.

Place names Admiralty charts and sailing directions follow the Ordnance Survey convention of printing academic renderings of Gaelic names, with a variety of accents as they would appear in a Gaelic dictionary. Some of these are quite unpronounceable other than by Gaelic speakers (and, I believe, sometimes unrecognisable even to them). Both authorities sometimes use anglicised versions, or translations of Gaelic words, apparently quite arbitrarily; for example you may come across 'Old Woman Rock' among a patch of Gaelic names on a chart, or alternatively a Gaelic name alongside its equivalent anglicisation. The early surveyors often made up their own names, based on natural features, their own translations of the Gaelic, or events or personalities connected with the survey, and these names were used on earlier charts, but have not often survived. Some names (such as Wreck Bay on Bute) are only used by yachtsmen.

Place names need to be communicated verbally, for example between the navigator, helmsman and lookout, so I have used the popular form of a name where there is one, as well as the name which appears on current charts. The spelling of these names matches that on the Admiralty charts, less any accents. You may find some discrepancies, but I hope they will not be so great as to cause confusion. See Appendix II.

Emergencies

Serious and immediate emergencies (including medical ones) are usually best referred to the coastguard. If you don't have VHF R/T but are able to get ashore (for example, if a crew member is ill), phone the coastguard or police. For less serious problems, such as a mechanical breakdown out of range of a boatyard, mechanics experienced at least with tractor or fishing-boat engines, will often be found locally.

Coastguard The Maritime Rescue Co-ordination Centre for the area is Clyde Coastguard, ☎ (0475) 29988.

Lifeboats are stationed, within the limits of this volume, at Portpatrick, Girvan, Troon, Campbeltown and Port Askaig. There are inshore rescue boats at Largs and Rhu.

Notes on plans and pilotage directions

Generally the conventions used on Admiralty charts have been followed so that this pilot may be used in conjunction with them. Please see under *Charts* on page 1.

Passages are described as far as possible for an approach from seaward, but this is not possible in the case of sounds between islands, and the Kyles of Bute have been taken from east to west, and Kilbrannan Sound from north to south to fit in with a continuous sequence of chapters.

In each chapter information relating to the whole chapter about charts, tides, marks and dangers, comes first; then any passage directions, sometimes including certain anchorages where it is necessary to relate these to plans associated with the passages; then any branches from the main passage; and finally individual anchorages, usually in the same sequence as the passages described.

Conspicuous features are listed particularly to help identification in poor visibility.

Lights, and any directions for making a passage or approach by night, are separated from the description of dangers and marks, as most of us sail by day for most of the time, and this reduces the information to be absorbed.

Bearings are from seaward and refer to true north. A few of the plans are not orientated with north at the top in order to make the best use of the space available, but reference to the north point will make this clear.

Distances are given in nautical miles and cables (tenths of nautical mile); less than ¼ cable is generally expressed in metres.

Depths and heights are given in metres to correspond with the current Admiralty charts. Depths are related to the current chart datum which is generally lower than that on older charts. It is the lowest level to which the surface of the sea is expected to fall owing to astronomical causes. If high barometric pressure and/or strong offshore winds coincide with a low spring tide the water may fall below this level, in which case there will be less depth than shown on the chart, or sketch plan.

Tides Heights of tides are represented by five figures; these are: Mean High Water Springs, Mean High Water Neaps, Mean Tide Level, Mean Low Water Neaps, Mean Low Water Springs. The word *Mean* is important because (for example) Low Water Springs in any particular fortnight may be substantially higher or lower than the mean. If you have tide tables which give heights of tides at Greenock or Oban (depending on whether you are east or west of Kintyre) you will be able to relate the height of tide on any particular day to the mean figures there (4·0 2·9 2·4 1·8 0·7 for Oban, 3·4 2·9 1·9 1·0 0·4 for Greenock) and judge whether the rise and fall is greater or less than the mean.

The difference between times of tides at Greenock or Oban and at Dover may vary by as much as 40 minutes, so that local tide tables will give more accurate results than those for Dover. In addition to Admiralty tide tables and commercial almanacs, pocket tide tables for Greenock and Oban are supplied by local chandlers, boatyards and marinas. Times and heights of high water at both ports are also included in the *Clyde Cruising Club Yearbook*. A new almanac published annually from 1989 is the *Malin, Hebrides and Minches Edition* of the *Yachtsman's Almanac*, available from chandlers or post-free from the publishers, Clyde Marine Press, Westgate, Toward, Argyll PA23 7UA, at £7.50.

Plans of anchorages and passages in this pilot are often at a larger scale than those on current charts, and the information in them is compiled from many sources. These include the Admiralty's original surveys; air photographs mostly of RAF origin; observations by other yachtsmen; and my own surveys, both from the air and by sea, as well as from land. Some of them are based directly on British Admiralty charts, with the permission of the Hydrographer of the Navy.

Photographs and views from sea level are used to illustrate transits and clearing marks, or to help identify landmarks, while air and hilltop photos often show more detail than can be included in the plans. Transits are in some cases more clearly illustrated when the marks used are not actually aligned; where this is done the marks are indicated by pointers.

Key to symbols used on plans

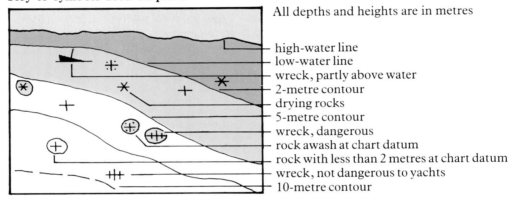

All depths and heights are in metres

- high-water line
- low-water line
- wreck, partly above water
- 2-metre contour
- drying rocks
- 5-metre contour
- wreck, dangerous
- rock awash at chart datum
- rock with less than 2 metres at chart datum
- wreck, not dangerous to yachts
- 10-metre contour

I. Firth of Clyde approaches

The distance from the Mull of Galloway to Heads of Ayr is about 55 miles. In that distance there is one natural inlet, a couple of harbours neither of which is accessible at low water or in strong onshore winds, and a few smaller harbours accessible only to shoal-draught boats.

Passages round the Mull of Kintyre are discussed in Chapter V.

Charts

2198 (1:75,000), *2126* (1:75,000), OS map *82*

Tides

In the middle of North Channel tidal streams run at up to 4 knots along the line of the channel. The southeast-going stream begins about +0440 Greenock (+0600 Dover), and the northwest-going stream begins about −0120 Greenock (HW Dover).

South of the Mull of Galloway for several miles streams run at up to 4 knots in an east-west direction. The east-going stream begins about +0530 Greenock (−0545 Dover) and the west-going stream begins about −0030 Greenock (+0045 Dover). Eddies run SSE along the shore of the Rhins south of Portpatrick.

Passage notes

The passage from the Irish Sea to the Firth of Clyde is generally straightforward except near the Mull of Galloway when there are eddies and overfalls. The passage round the Mull of Kintyre is described in Chapter V.

Lights

At night the approach to the Firth of Clyde is well lit except that Ailsa Craig light is obscured over a wide sector on its west side. Look out for other traffic, particularly fishing and naval vessels which may not maintain a steady course and speed. The following are the major lights in the approach to the Clyde (parts of this list are repeated where relevant to sections of the coast but are included here for the benefit of a yacht approaching the Clyde at night):

Mull of Galloway lighthouse Fl.20s99m28M
Crammag Head lighthouse Fl.10s35m18M
Killantringan Head lighthouse Fl(2)15s49m25M
Group of four radio masts 5 miles north of Portpatrick with red obstruction lights
Corsewall Point Al.LFl.WR.74s34m18M
Ailsa Craig Fl(6)30s18m17M (028°-obscd-145°)
Turnberry Point Fl.15s29m24M

Pladda (south of Arran) Fl(3)30s40m23M
Pillar Rock Point (east of Arran) Fl(2)20s38m25M
Lady Isle (southwest of Troon) Fl(4)30s19m8M
Sanda Island (south of Kintyre) LFl.WR.24s50m 19/16M
Island Davaar (east of Kintyre) Fl(2)10s37m23M

Shelter

East Tarbert Bay, on the east side of the Mull of Galloway, provides shelter from the west but strong tides and very heavy seas off the Mull itself may make the approach hazardous when shelter is most needed.

Loch Ryan is easily entered although there may be heavy seas under some conditions off the west side of the entrance.

Lamlash Bay on the east shore of Arran provides shelter around its shores and is easily entered by day or night.

The Rhins of Galloway

The hammerhead peninsula of the Rhins, 26 miles long, has an inhospitable rocky coast with a few bays and the partly ruined harbour of Portpatrick. There are many groups of radio masts on the Rhins.

Chart

2198 (1:75,000), OS map *82*

Tides

Eddies and overfalls occur inshore along the coast of the Rhins. The south-going stream begins about +0310 Greenock (+0430 Dover), and the north-going stream begins about −0250 Greenock (−0310 Dover), running at up to 5 knots at springs south of Black Head, decreasing further north to 2 knots at Corsewall Point.

Dangers and marks

There are no hidden dangers affecting a yacht on passage in good visibility outwith a cable from the shore. About 2¼ miles southwest of Corsewall Point the drying rock Craig Laggan, two cables from the shore, is marked by a stone beacon with a blunt pointed top. The main landmarks on the Rhins of Galloway are:

Mull of Galloway lighthouse at the south end of the Mull of Galloway, a white tower 26 metres high on top of a cliff.

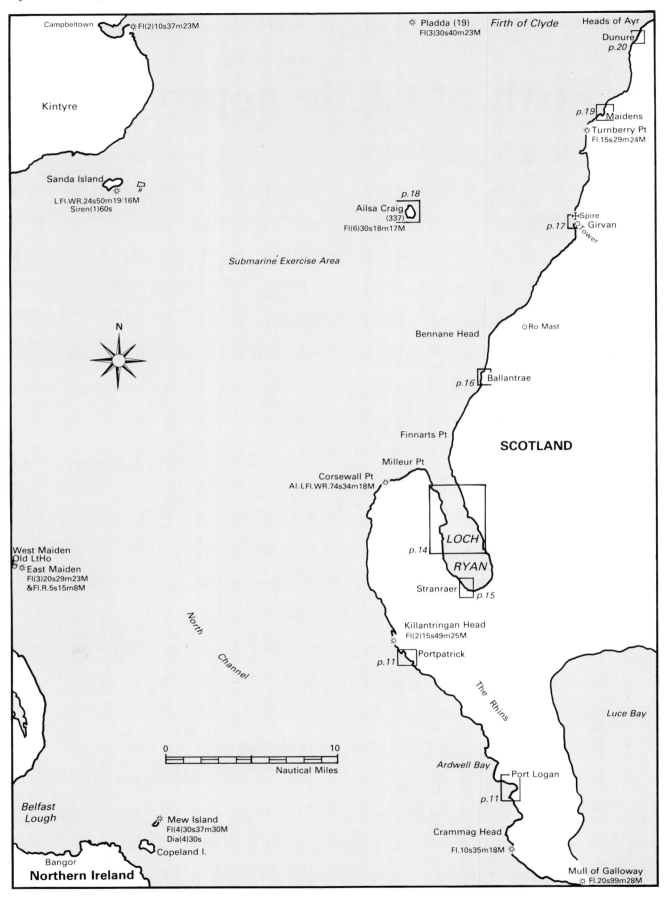

Campbeltown · Fl(2)10s37m23M

Kintyre

Sanda Island ·
L Fl.WR.24s50m19/16M
Siren(1)60s

· Pladda (19)
Fl(3)30s40m23M   *Firth of Clyde*   Heads of Ayr

Dunure
p.20

p.19 · Maidens

· Turnberry Pt
Fl.15s29m24M

p.18
Ailsa Craig
(337)
Fl(6)30s18m17M

Submarine Exercise Area

† Spire
p.17 · Girvan
Tower

○ Ro Mast

Bennane Head

N

p.16 · Ballantrae

Finnarts Pt

SCOTLAND

Milleur Pt

Corsewall Pt ·
Al.LFl.WR.74s34m18M

p.14   *LOCH*

RYAN

West Maiden
Old LtHo
○·East Maiden
Fl(3)20s29m23M
&Fl.R.5s15m8M

Stranraer   *p.15*

North

Channel

Killantringan Head
Fl(2)15s49m25M

·
p.11 · Portpatrick

The Rhins

Luce Bay

0   10

Nautical Miles

Ardwell Bay   Port Logan

p.11

*Belfast
Lough*

· Mew Island
Fl(4)30s37m30M
Dia(4)30s
Copeland I.

Crammag Head

Fl.10s35m18M ·

Bangor

Northern Ireland

Mull of Galloway
· Fl.20s99m28M

Crammag Head lighthouse, 4 miles WNW of Mull of Galloway, a 6 metre white tower 30 metres above sea level.

Portpatrick village 10 miles south of Corsewall Point, with a single radio mast with dish aerials on it behind the village.

Killantringan Head lighthouse, 1½ miles northwest of Portpatrick, a 22-metre white tower at sea level.

Various groups of radio masts in the northern part of the Rhins are easily confused with each other, but the principal group of four masts is a mile inland, 5 miles north of Portpatrick.

Corsewall Point lighthouse at the north end of the Rhins, a 34-metre white tower.

Lights

Mull of Galloway lighthouse Fl.20s99m28M
Crammag Head lighthouse, Fl.10s35m18M
Killantringan Head lighthouse, Fl(2)15s49m25M
Group of four radio masts 5 miles north of Port-patrick with red obstruction lights
Corsewall Point Al.LFl.WR.74s34m18M

Occasional anchorages

Port Logan Bay, 54°43'·5N 4°58'W, 3½ miles north of Crammag Head, has moderate depths for anchoring offshore. A stone breakwater 180 metres long on the south side of the bay provides shelter for small shoal-draught boats able to take the ground.

Ardwell Bay, 54°46'N 5°00'W, nearly 3 miles further north, provides shelter in offshore winds.

Portpatrick

54°50'·5N 5°07'W

Attempts were made in the late 18th and early 19th centuries to develop a harbour here for Irish traffic, but the breakwaters were destroyed by the sea, and the harbour was formally abandoned about 1870 with the coming of steamships able to negotiate the length of Loch Ryan.

The entrance is 35 metres wide between low water lines, with ruined breakwaters on both sides, a broad drying rocky shore on its south side and several drying rocks on the north side, the most easterly of which, Half Tide Rock, is marked by a floating oil drum. The Inner Harbour is small, but it is popular with Irish crews, especially at weekends.

From northwest the entrance is not easily identified until it is abeam. A single radio mast east of the village has many dish aerials on it, and there is a single plain mast close north of the village.

From south the hotel on the north side of harbour is conspicuous.

Once inside shelter is good although with strong southwest winds some sea may work in even to the inner harbour. Outside the inner harbour there is only 0·5 metre in the channel.

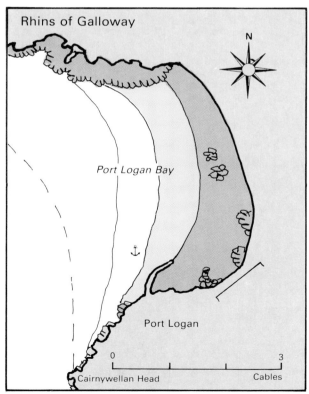

Rhins of Galloway

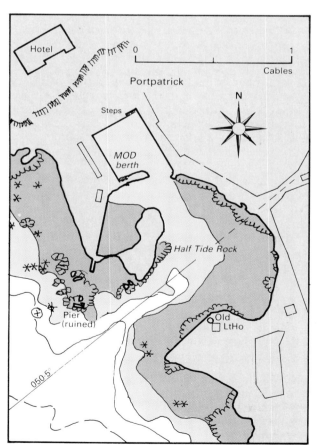

Portpatrick

Portpatrick entrance from the south shore. The ruined North Pier is on the left, McCook's Craig to the right and the conspicuous hotel on the hill behind. The channel is only 35 metres wide between LW lines.

Portpatrick harbour from the south shore. The disused lighthouse is on the right and the entrance to the inner harbour on the left.

Tides

Tides run at over 4 knots northwest and southeast 2 cables off the entrance.

Constant +0022 Liverpool (+0037 Dover)

Height in metres

MHWS	MHWN	MTL	MLWN	MLWS
3·8	3·0	2·0	0·9	0·3

Approach

The harbour should not be approached within 2 hours of LW, more if there is any onshore sea, owing to the shoal depth in the approach to the inner harbour. It is essential to pick up the leading marks: an orange vertical stripe on the harbour wall and another on the left-hand corner of a building in the main street 050·5°, as illustrated.

As soon as the inner harbour opens up to port bear round to that side to avoid the drying sandy bay to starboard. The only berths are in the inner harbour, the southwest side of which is reserved for a Ministry of Defence patrol boat. A lifeboat lies to moorings in the middle of the inner harbour. Avoid mooring in front of stone steps; you will be asked to move.

Lights

At night F.G lights are lit on the leading line, but usually only on demand and their existence cannot be relied on.

Supplies

Shops, post office, telephones, hotels, *Calor Gas*, petrol, diesel at Esso garage in main street, water at inner harbour, EC Thursday. Harbourmaster ☎ (077 681) 355.

The Inner Harbour. The lifeboat is on a mooring to left of centre.

Portpatrick leading line from McCook's Craig. The front mark is a faded orange stripe on the sea wall, and the back mark is also an orange stripe, on the left-hand corner of the gable of the low two-storey house with three windows in it, to the left of the front mark in this photo. They must be kept very carefully in line.

Loch Ryan

Loch Ryan provides the best and most accessible shelter south of Troon. The approach is straightforward but there may be heavy seas off Milleur Point at the west side of the entrance, especially in northwest winds with an ebb tide.

The inner part of the loch is shallow with a drying spit (The Spit) extending southeast for over a mile from the west side of the loch, providing some shelter in the bay behind it, known as The Wig.

Car ferries run to Larne from Loch Ryan, both from Stranraer and Cairnryan, and naval vessels also berth occasionally at Cairnryan.

Chart

1403 (1:10,000), OS map *82*

Tides

The stream turns northwest about HW Greenock (+0115 Dover) and southeast about 5½ hours later running at 1½ knots at springs.

Constant −0020 Greenock (+0055 Dover)

Height in metres

MHWS	MHWN	MTL	MLWN	MLWS
3·0	2·5	1·6	0·6	0·2

Dangers and marks

The principal mark is Cairn Point lighthouse on the east shore.

Cairn Point from a hillside, looking south towards Stranraer. A car ferry on the left has just entered the dredged channel which is marked by light beacons.

Milleur Point, the west point of the entrance, has a north cardinal buoy 3 cables NNE of it, a drying rock a cable off the point and another a cable offshore ½ mile SSE of the point.

Jamieson's Point is the most prominent feature of the west shore, 1½ miles SSE of Milleur Point. Rocks drying and submerged extend over 4 cables from the west shore south of Jamieson's Point, merging with The Spit.

In mid-channel, between Jamieson's Point and Cairn Point, port and starboard-hand light buoys mark underwater hazards recently discovered by ferries but of no concern to yachts.

The Spit extends over a mile southeast from Kirkcolm Point opposite Cairn Point, its outer end marked by *Spit* G conical light buoy.

South of the *Spit* buoy three green light beacons mark the west edge of the channel to Stranraer Harbour. Yachts can sail outwith the channel and should give way to ferries or any other large vessels confined to the channel.

Agnew Monument is on the skyline west of the loch.

Anchoring is prohibited in the fairway off Cairn Point, and between the fairway and the east shore from ½ mile north of Cairn Point to 2 cables south of the light beacon at Cairnryan Ferry Terminal; also in the channel on the east side of beacons 1 to 5 and in the area northwest of the East Pier at Stranraer where the ferries turn round.

Approach

Keep a lookout for ferry and other traffic and keep well off the west shore as Cairn Point is approached; pass east of *Spit* buoy.

Lights

Milleur Point north cardinal buoy Q
Buoys NNW of Cairn Point Fl.R.5s and Fl.G.5s
Cairn Point lighthouse Fl(2)R.10s14m12M
Cairnryan Ferry Terminal Fl.R.5s5m5M with F.G and F.R lights inshore.
Spit buoy Fl.G.6s
No. 1 beacon Oc.G.6s
No. 3 beacon Q.G
No. 5 beacon Fl.G.3s

Anchorages

The Wig on the west shore provides some shelter from northeast behind The Spit. From *Spit* buoy head southwest with Agnew monument on the skyline 030° on the starboard bow for ½ mile, west for ½ mile, then northwest towards moored yachts. Anchor off sailing club slip clear of moorings or, in northeast winds, as far up to north shore as depth and swinging room allow. Loch Ryan Sailing Club is at the head of the concrete slip.

The sailing club welcomes visiting yachts and can provide showers when the clubhouse is open; there is usually someone about on Wednesday evenings and Saturday and Sunday afternoons. Keep clear of yachts which may be racing.

In strong winds from south to southeast The Wig is uncomfortable and Stranraer Harbour is better; north to northwest winds send a swell into the harbour and The Wig then provides better shelter.

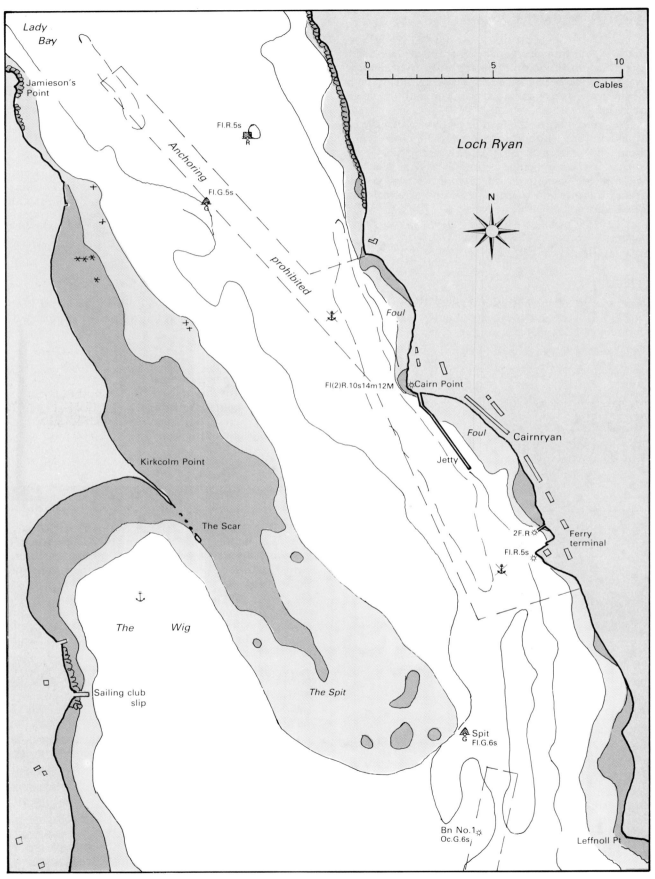

Lady Bay

Jamieson's Point

Fl.R.5s R

Fl.G.5s

Anchoring

prohibited

0   5   10

Cables

Loch Ryan

N

Foul

Fl(2)R.10s14m12M ☆Cairn Point

Foul   Cairnryan

Jetty

Kirkcolm Point

The Scar

2F.R ☆   Ferry terminal

Fl.R.5s ☆

The   Wig

Sailing club slip

The Spit

Spit
G Fl.G.6s

Bn No.1 ☆
Oc.G.6s

Leffnoll Pt

Loch Ryan

14

Stranraer Harbour

Stranraer Harbour consists of three piers of which the East and Centre piers are reserved for RoRo ferries. Small craft moor on the east side of the root of West Pier, but there is only 1 metre in the entrance channel which is marked by a floating oil drum on each side.

The beacon northwest of the head of West Pier is a pole on a concrete base; when the base is showing there is less than 1·7 metres in the entrance.

Make fast at the inner end of West Pier, south of the 'knuckle' and find the harbourmaster, whose office is at the base of a clock tower at the head of the harbour.

Alternatively anchor outside the harbour northwest of West Pier, clear of the prohibited area and clear of the outfall pipe, and rocks inshore.

Stranraer Harbour from the head of the East Pier. Middle Pier is on the left and West Pier to the right with the harbour between them.

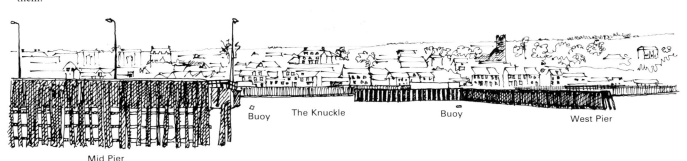

Mid Pier   Buoy   The Knuckle   Buoy   West Pier

Lights

At night the approach beacons are lit and the harbour has a colourful display of fixed lights to try to show up against the shore lights:

No. 1 beacon Oc.G.6s
No. 3 beacon Q.G
No. 5 beacon Fl.G.3s
East Pier 2F.R(vert)9m
Centre Pier 2F.Bu(vert)
West Pier head 2F.G(vert)10m4M
West Pier knuckle 2F.G(vert)5m4M

Supplies

Shops, post office, bank, phones, hotels, *Calor Gas*, petrol, diesel at garage, water, EC Wednesday.

Communications

Harbour office ☎ (0776) 2460. VHF Ch 16, 14 (24hr).

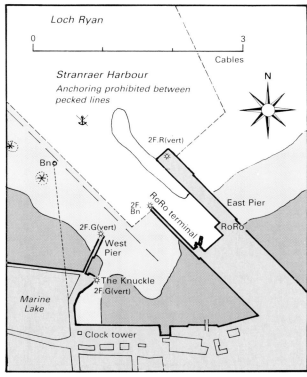

Stranraer

Occasional anchorages in Loch Ryan

Lady Bay 1½ miles inside the entrance on the west side of the loch and 4 cables NNW of Jamieson's Point.

Finnarts Bay, at the mouth of Glenapp, opposite Lady Bay, may be better in easterly winds, but fierce squalls are likely to come from the glen.

Loch Ryan to Heads of Ayr

Charts

2199, 2126 (1:75,000). Of these *2126* is the most useful particularly if a passage to or round Kintyre is envisaged. OS maps *70, 76*.

Tides

Tidal streams are not significant except close inshore.

Dangers and marks

Between Corsewall Point and Arran there are no hidden dangers in reasonable visibility outwith ½ mile from the shore.

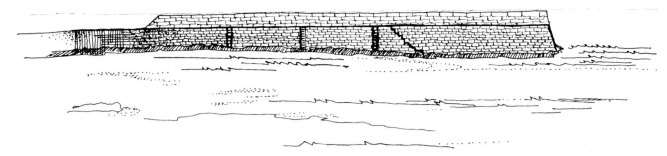

Ballantrae Pier from north.

Ailsa Craig, 55°15′N 5°07′W, 11 miles south of Arran, 337 metres high, is the principal reference point.

Turnberry Point, 55°20′N 4°50′W, a white lighthouse 24 metres high.

Culzean Castle, 55°21′N 4°47′W, an ornate building on a cliff 3 miles northeast of Turnberry Point.

Occasional anchorages

Ballantrae, 55°06′N 5°00′W, about halfway between Corsewall Point and Girvan, is most easily identified by Knockdollan, a conspicuous conical hill 3 miles northeast of the village. A stone pier which dries, at the north end of the village, provides some shelter from south at high water or to boats which can take the ground. Access to the drying basin at the pier is obstructed by mooring lines for lobster and angling boats. Supplies in the village.

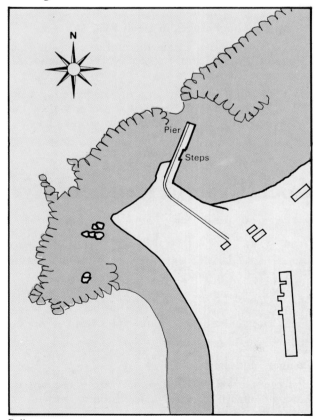

Ballantrae

Girvan

55°14′·5N 4°51′·5W

The most attractive harbour on the east side of the Clyde, but difficult to enter owing to shoaling of the channel, although there are proposals for permanent improvements. Girvan is often crowded with fishing boats and berthing for yachts is limited.

Chart

Plan on *1866* (1:6,250)

Tides

Constant −0032 Greenock (+0043 Dover)

Height in metres

MHWS	MHWN	MTL	MLWN	MLWS
3·1	2·6	1·8	0·9	0·4

Dangers and marks

Depths in the entrance vary owing to movement of the bottom. Girvan Patch, with a least depth of 1·7 metres, 4 cables SSW of the entrance and 4 cables offshore, is a hazard if approaching from south, as are drying reefs 1½ cables SSW of the entrance.

Northwest winds cause heavy seas in the entrance, and there is a strong current from the river after heavy rain.

The head of the North Breakwater is marked by a light beacon.

Unless the depth on the bar is known enter only within 3 hours of high water. Keep closer to the South Pier than to the North Breakwater.

A screen jetty keeps debris from the river away from the South Pier, which is used by fishing boats.

Moor temporarily on the south side of the screen jetty and find the harbourmaster in order to be allocated a suitable berth.

Traffic signals

Signals are shown at the east end of the South Pier; by day two black discs horizontally disposed, at night two red lights, indicate that the harbour is closed.

Girvan from southwest. Since this photo was taken the North Breakwater has been rebuilt; the beacon at its head shows beyond the head of South Pier which is in the foreground.

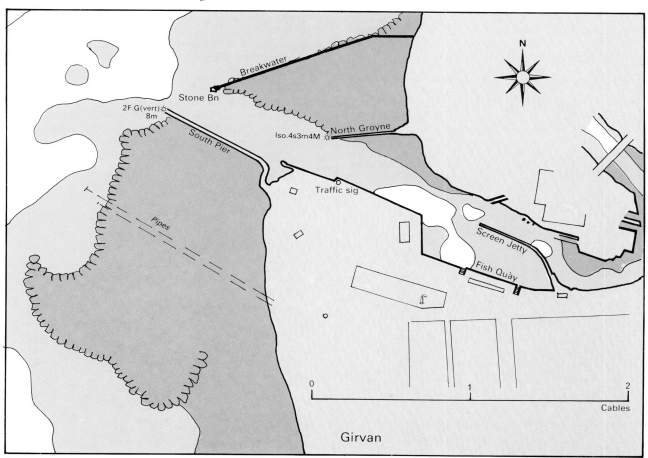

Girvan

Lights

South Pier 2F.G(vert)8m4M
North Breakwater Fl(2)R.6s7m4M
North Groyne Iso.4s3m4M
2F.R(horiz) at South Pier indicate harbour closed.

Supplies and services

Shops, post office, telephone, bank, hotel, *Calor Gas*, petrol, diesel, water, EC Wednesday, Indoor swimming pool. Boatbuilder: Alex Nobles and Sons Ltd, ☎ (0465) 2223. Girvan Chandlers ☎ (0465) 2897.

Communications

Harbour office ☎ (0465) 3048. VHF Ch 16, 12 (0900–1700, Mon–Fri).

Ailsa Craig, 55°15′N 5°07′W, 8 miles offshore, is steep-to all round but a timber jetty on its northeast side has a depth of 0·6 metre at its head. Depths are suitable for anchoring in very quiet weather close inshore northwest of the jetty but beware of the ruins of an old jetty close west of the existing jetty. Use a tripping line as the steeply shelving bottom consists of granite boulders under which an anchor may be jammed.

Ask the lighthouse keepers whether a supply boat or helicopter is expected; a yacht should not in any case be left unattended, either at anchor or alongside. The light is to be automated in 1990.

Ailsa Craig from northeast. The jetty is on the right-hand side of the spit in the foreground.

Maidens

55°20′N 4°49′W

Maidens is a drying harbour on the south side of Maidenhead Bay, 1½ miles northeast of Turnberry lighthouse, which can be entered in settled conditions by yachts able to take the ground, but it is fairly fully occupied by local boats and there may not be any space alongside the quay. The harbour is formed by a stone quay and breakwater connecting a line of rocks on its west side, and an incomplete breakwater on its east side. The channel within the harbour is marked by iron beacons.

Keown Rock in the middle of the bay, ¼ mile north of the harbour entrance, covers at half tide. Temporary anchorage can be found in 2 metres between Keown Rock and the harbour entrance.

Shops, post office, telephone, hotel, *Calor Gas* at caravan site, petrol, diesel at garage, water.

Harbourmaster (part time) (065 53) 478.

Culzean Bay provides temporary anchorage in settled weather in 5 metres.

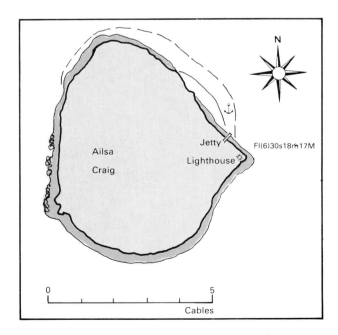

Ailsa
Craig

Jetty
Lighthouse
Fl(6)30s18m17M

N

0   5
Cables

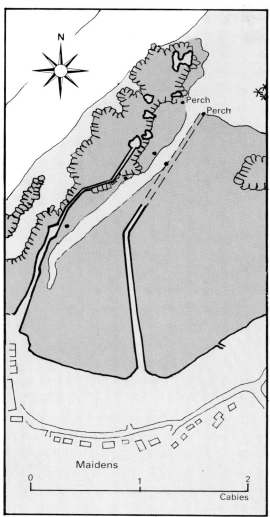

Maidens

The entrance channel at Maidens from the head of the harbour, showing the perches on either hand, Keown Rock beyond, and Barwhin Point. The point at top left is at the north side of Culzean Bay.

Maidens Harbour from northwest, near high tide.

Dunure from southwest. The castle is at bottom right.

Dunure

55°24′·5N 4°45′·5W

A small artificial drying harbour 2 miles southwest of the Heads of Ayr, foul with small-boat moorings, Dunure is identified by a ruined castle on the shore at the south end of the village, and the harbour is identified by the stone beacon on the breakwater. It should only be attempted if there is no sea running and at not less than half-flood, and only by a boat able to take the ground, unless for a very brief stay.

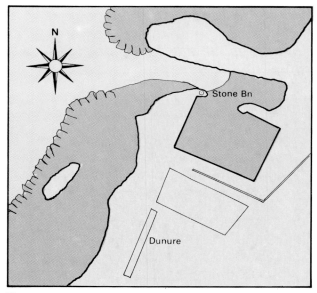

Dunure

Dunure from above the head of the harbour.

II. Firth of Clyde

Traffic in the Firth of Clyde has diminished in recent years, but a sharp lookout needs to be kept for naval vessels (especially submarines) and fishing boats, all of which may behave unpredictably, and very large tankers and bulk carriers.

Charts

2126 (1:75,000), *2220* (1:36,000)

Shelter

Lamlash Bay on the east side of Arran provides shelter around its shores and is easily entered by day or night.

Troon is the only artificial harbour on the east side of the Clyde south of Cumbrae Islands which is accessible in strong onshore winds. However, in strong southwesterly winds there may be heavy seas on the shoals with nowhere to run for, and in these conditions Lamlash is a better refuge.

Largs Yacht Haven provides shelter and the approach itself is sheltered and well lit, but there is little space to enter under sail.

Marks

Heads of Ayr, a dark cliff about 80 metres high on the south side of Ayr Bay; a group of 3 radio masts stands on Bron Carrick Hill about 1½ miles south of Heads of Ayr.

A yellow spherical light buoy is moored 4 miles west of Heads of Ayr.

Lady Isle, 55°31'·5N 4°44'W, 2 miles southwest of Troon Point, is 3 metres high and has a white tapering light beacon 16 metres in height.

Ailsa Shipyard shed at Troon, 35 metres high, shows as a pale rectangle from a long way off.

A new paper mill, a long light-coloured building a mile north of Troon is more conspicuous than the Ailsa shed, especially in afternoon or evening light.

A 136-metre chimney 2 miles northwest of Irvine harbour entrance is conspicuous in clear weather.

Horse Island, northwest of Ardrossan, has a single tapering beacon on it but it is stone coloured and the island is close inshore.

Dangers

Unmarked rocks, submerged and drying, extend over half a mile from the shore between the Heads of Ayr and Irvine, and between Ardrossan and Farland Head.

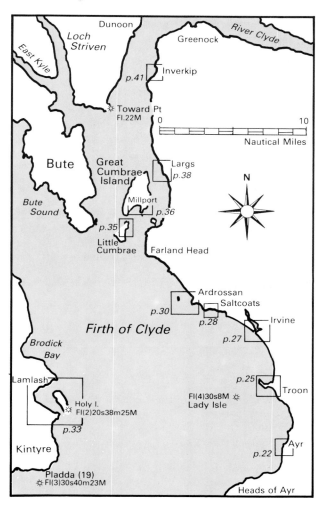

The shallowest part of Saltpan Spit, with a depth of 1·6 metres 1¾ miles NNW of Ayr harbour entrance, can be avoided by keeping the 136-metre chimney north of Irvine open west of Troon Point 345°.

Black Rocks, drying 6 cables from the shore 2 miles SSE of Troon, are charted as having a beacon near their south end, but it was missing in May 1988.

Lady Isle has drying rocks all round it, up to 2 cables to the northeast.

Lappock Rock 1½ miles north of Troon has a stone tower on it.

Yellow light buoys in Irvine Bay 1–1½ miles offshore are of no significance to yachts but may provide a useful check on position.

By remaining outwith the 15-metre contour a yacht will keep clear of these dangers, but several isolated shoals outwith this depth will puzzle any navigator who is relying on his echo sounder and has not kept his track on the chart. Passing Ardrossan the 15-metre contour is the closest distance at which it is safe to be from the land, and west of Horse Island a 6-metre shoal will be found on this line.

Lights

At night there are no major lights on the east shore and harbour lights are difficult to see against lights ashore.

Yellow buoy 4 miles west of Heads of Ayr Fl.Y.10s
Lady Isle Fl(4)30s19m8M

Harbour lights are shown under the respective harbours.

Ayr

55°28′N 4°38′W

A commercial harbour devoted to fish and scrap metal, but supporting an enthusiastic yacht club. The entrance is straightforward except in strong onshore winds when it should be avoided.

Chart

Plan on *1866* (1:10,000)

Tides

Constant −0025 Greenock (+0050 Dover)

Height in metres

MHWS	MHWN	MTL	MLWN	MLWS
3·0	2·6	1·8	1·1	0·5

Dangers and marks

A dark gasholder with a light grey top at the north end of the town, and a spire south of the harbour entrance, are conspicuous.

St Nicholas Rock and submerged rocks extending ¼ mile WSW of the south pierhead are marked by a starboard-hand light buoy, *Outer St Nicholas*, 4 cables west of the south pierhead.

Traffic signals

Signals are shown from a mast at the outer end of North Quay, two cables within the entrance: two black balls vertically disposed by day; two red lights by night indicating that the harbour is closed.

Entrance

Pass north of *Outer St Nicholas* buoy and between the South Pier and the North Breakwater. Ayr Yacht and Cruising Club have moorings in a dock on the south side of the river; turn to starboard as soon as the dock opens up; pick up a vacant moor-

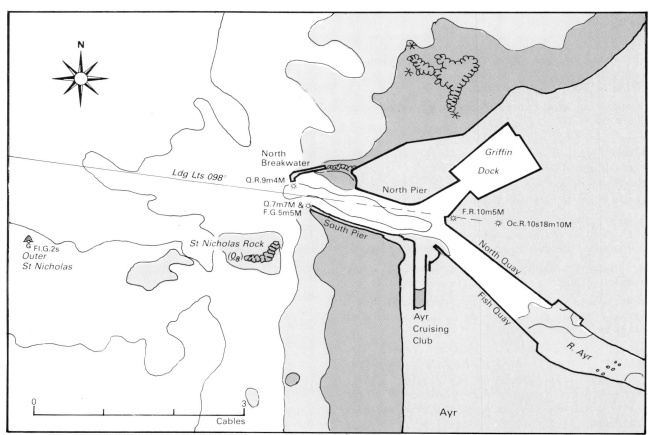

Ayr

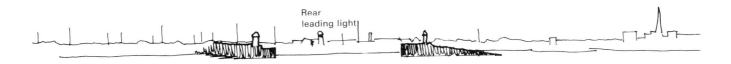

Ayr Harbour approach.

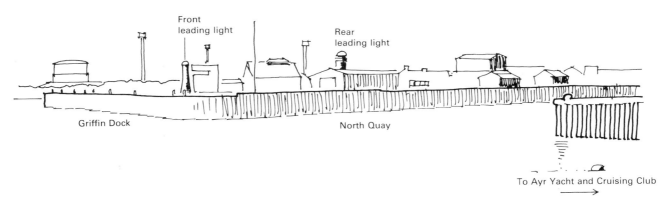

Ayr Harbour.

Lady Isle from westward.

ing temporarily and ask the club staff or members for advice. If a floating pontoon is in position on the east side of the dock, go alongside there. Alternatively, make fast temporarily at the west end of the North Quay and call at the harbour office.

Before entering harbour call the harbourmaster on VHF to find out whether any large vessels are moving.

Lights

Outer St Nicholas buoy Fl.G.2s

South Pier Q.7m7M, with F.G.5m5M showing southwest over St Nicholas Rock, but part of water over which the F.G light does not show has less than 1·5 metres

North Breakwater Q.R.7m5M

Leading lights 098° front F.R.10m5M and rear Oc.R.10s18m9M

Traffic signals (as above) 2F.R(vert) at North Breakwater indicate that the harbour is closed.

Supplies and services

Shops, post office, bank, telephone, hotel, *Calor Gas*, petrol, diesel, water, EC Wednesday.

Repairs to hull, machinery and electrics: J. W. Mackay ☎ (0292) 281586. Ship chandlers: J. Goodwin ☎ (0292) 263837.

Communications

Harbour office at North Quay: ☎ (0292) 281687, VHF Ch 14.

Troon

55°33′N 4°41′W

The easiest harbour to approach on this coast, identified by 35-metre-high sheds of Ailsa Shipbuilding Yard. Troon Marina is in the inner harbour.

Chart

Plan on *1866* (1:6,250)

Tides

Constant −0025 Greenock (+0050 Dover)

Height in metres

MHWS	MHWN	MTL	MLWN	MLWS
3·1	2·6	1·8	0·9	0·4

Dangers and marks

Strong southwest winds build up very heavy seas in the approach and in these conditions it may be better to make for Lamlash or Largs Marina. Troon Rock, a mile west of the entrance, breaks in heavy weather. Heavy seas build up in the entrance in strong northwest winds. There is space for a sailing

Troon from north.

Troon Harbour entrance from southwest.

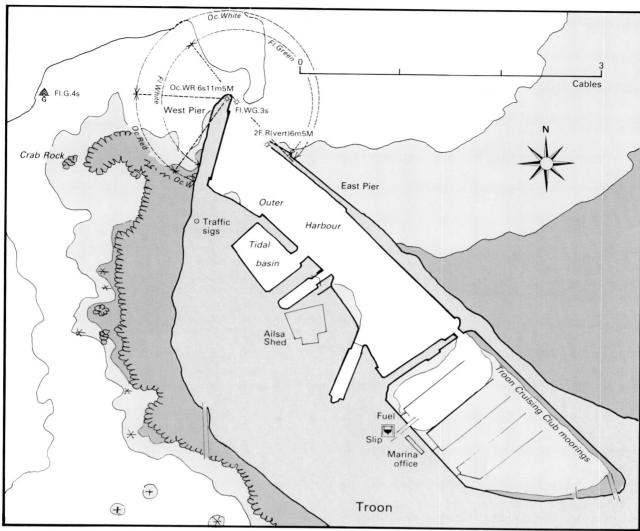

Troon

yacht to round up inside the entrance to drop sails, if essential.

Lady Isle, 3 metres high with a white tapered light beacon, lies 2 miles southwest of the entrance, with rocks and shoals all round, up to 2 cables to the northeast.

Crab Rock over a cable west of West Pier is marked by a starboard-hand light buoy a cable northwest of the rock.

Mill Rock which dries 0·4m, 4 cables NNE of the entrance, is marked on its south side by an unlit rusty can buoy.

Lappock Rock, 1½ miles north of the entrance, is marked by a stone tower.

Approach

From south or west identify Crab Rock buoy and pass north of it. Coming from Ayr see clearing mark for Saltpan Spit above, page 21.

From north identify Mill Rock can buoy and pass clear west of it.

Watch out for naval and commercial traffic which may be hidden behind the entrance piers. If you have VHF call the marina on Ch M for advice, especially if traffic signals (see below) are showing.

Make for the inner harbour (note that the south part of the passage is obstructed by the sloping end of the wall separating the two parts of the harbour, marked by a perch and a line of flags), make fast temporarily at the outer end of the second pontoon, and report to the marina office. The tidal basin in the outer harbour is used by fishing boats but yachts may be able to berth there.

Traffic signals

By day two black balls vertically disposed on a mast a cable south of the north end of West Pier indicate that the harbour is closed.

Lights

Lady Isle Fl(4)30s19m8M
Crab Rock light buoy Fl.G.4s

West Pier shows Oc.WR.6s11m5M and Fl.WG.3s7m5M over the sectors shown on the plan

Outer end of East Pier has 2F.R(vert)6m5M

Traffic signals (as above) show 2F.R(vert) at night

The Fl.WG light at West Pier is not visible from southwest from the level of a yacht's deck; the 2F.R lights on East Pier have been listed as 'temporarily Fl.R.10s3M', and the 2F.R traffic signals are usually left switched on at night when there are no staff in the harbourmaster's office. From southwest keep outwith the 5-metre contour until in the white sector of the Oc.WR light.

Services and supplies

In town Shops, post office, bank, hotel, EC Wednesday.

At marina Telephone, *Calor Gas*, petrol, diesel, water, slip, hoist. Hull, mechanical and electrical repairs. Laundry, restaurant, bar, showers.

Communications

Marina ☎ (0292) 315553 VHF Ch M.
Harbourmaster ☎ (0292) 313412.

For Maritime Museum, Seaworld Centre and Leisure Centre, see Irvine below.

Irvine

55°36′N 4°42′W

A once thriving harbour principally devoted to exporting coal, but only a few buildings remain along the decaying wharves. The south side of the harbour has been 'landscaped' with a vast leisure centre and car parks.

Yachts are discouraged from entering the River Garnock, where there is a wharf for an explosives factory, operated by ICI, who also control the harbour.

The principal attractions are the shore birds which congregate on the mudflats, the Maritime Museum which is developing at pontoons on the south side of the River Irvine and ashore, Seaworld Centre which shows specimens of fish and sea creatures live in an aquarium, and the Magnum Leisure Centre.

Chart

Plan on *1866* (1:10,000)

Tides

Constant −0015 Greenock (+0100 Dover)

Height in metres

MHWS	MHWN	MTL	MLWN	MLWS
3·1	2·6	1·8	0·9	0·4

Tidal streams run across the entrance together with currents depending on winds. Also, during or after heavy rain a strong current flows out of the river.

Marks and dangers

The shallow river entrance has groynes on either side, marked by perches, with light beacons at the outer end of the channel. A white pilot tower at the entrance is conspicuous.

There is some commercial traffic to Garnock wharf, and commercial vessels occasionally use the wharf on the south side.

Yellow light buoys in Irvine Bay 1–1½ miles offshore are of no significance to yachts but may provide a useful check on position.

Directions

The least depth on the bar is 0·1m, so that it should not be approached within 3 hours of LW or more if there is any sea. The leading marks are two tall lattice beacons on the south side of the river, east of the pilot tower, the front beacon is painted green and the rear one red. The leading line leads along the LW line on the southeast side of the channel.

Most of the quays on the south shore are derelict, but there is a sound section immediately west of the pontoons of the Maritime Museum with two small cranes on it and with good steel stairs recessed into its west end. Make fast there (not to the museum pontoons) and find the pilot whose office is in a cottage across the road from the cranes (for some reason the title of harbourmaster is held by someone in the office at the explosives factory).

Lights

Lappock Rock beacon is not lit
Entrance beacon northwest side Fl.R.3s6m5M
Entrance beacon southeast side Fl.G.3s6m5M
Leading lights 051° front F.G.10m5M and rear F.R.15m5M

Supplies

In town, ¾ mile, are Shops, post office, telephone, hotel, *Calor Gas*, petrol, diesel, water.

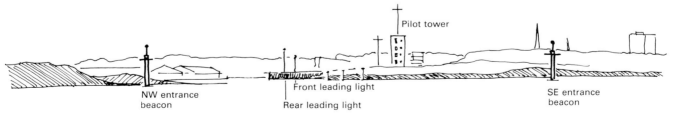

Irvine River entrance.

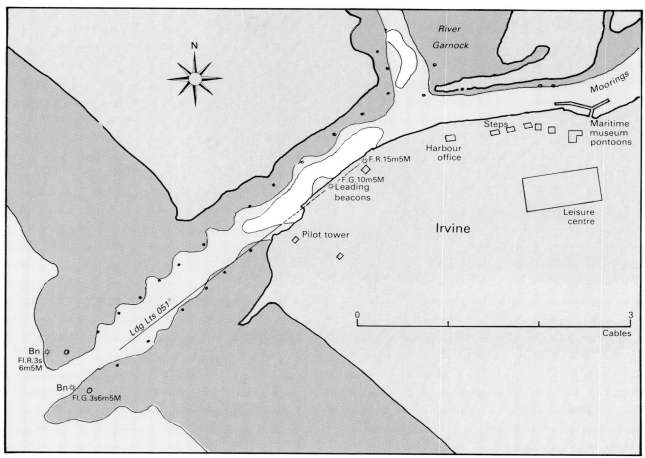

Irvine

Irvine River entrance from northwest.

Irvine harbour from northeast. The pontoons of the Maritime Museum are in the centre of the photo.

Communications

Pilot (harbour office) ☎ (0294) 311804.

Saltcoats

55°38′N 4°47′W

A small drying harbour built before 1700 and abandoned for commercial traffic, but now used by local small craft. Usual supplies and services in town.

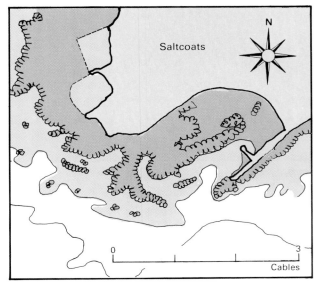

Saltcoats

Saltcoats Harbour.

Ardrossan

55°38'·5N 4°49'W

A commercial harbour in which yachts are not welcome, but which may provide shelter in exceptional circumstances, although the harbour is likely to be closed by southwest gales.

Chart

Plan on *1866* (1:7,500)

Tides

Constant −0010 Greenock (+0105 Dover)

Height in metres

MHWS	MHWN	MTL	MLWN	MLWS
3·2	2·7	1·9	1·1	0·5

Dangers and marks

Horse Isle, ½ mile WNW of the entrance, has a stone beacon at its south end.

West Crinan Rock, which dries 1·1 metres 1½ cables northwest of the harbour entrance, is marked by a red can light buoy.

Eagle Rock, just above water nearly 3 cables south of the entrance, is marked by a green conical light buoy on its west side.

The channel east of Horse Isle is obstructed by drying rocks, and drying reefs extend 1½ cables SSW of the island.

Approach and entrance

Pass at least 2 cables south of Horse Isle, identify the two buoys and pass between them. If you have VHF, call the harbourmaster before entering. The passage north of the breakwater is too obstructed with rocks to be considered.

Berth temporarily at steps by the harbourmaster's office on the north side of Eglinton Basin, which is on the southeast side of the harbour.

The north side of Montgomerie Pier which is 2 cables east of the entrance is a tanker berth, and both east and west sides of Winton Pier, southeast of the entrance, are car ferry terminals.

It is possible to anchor behind the breakwater, but the area inshore is shoal and drying, extending to the breakwater itself at its north end, so anchor close to the breakwater. It provides little shelter from southwest wind.

Traffic signals

When the harbour is closed 2 black balls vertically disposed are displayed at the west end of Montgomerie Pier by day (2F.R(vert) lights by night).

Ardrossan from northwest. Horse Isle in the foreground; a car ferry is in the harbour entrance.

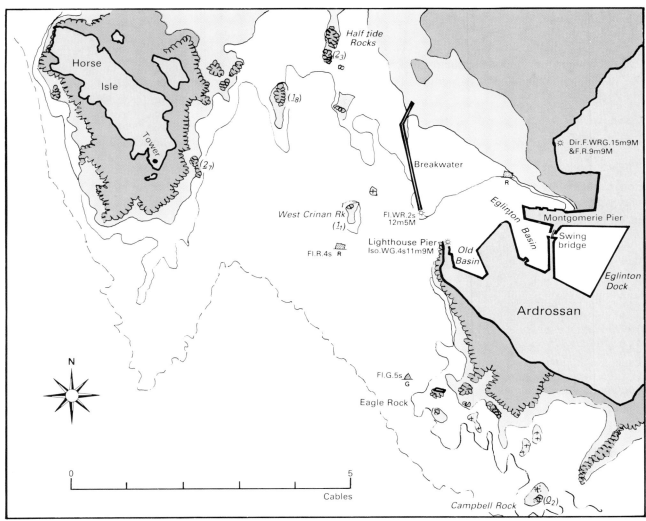

Ardrossan

Lights

Horse Isle beacon is not lit
West Crinan light buoy Fl.R.4s
Eagle Rock light buoy Fl.G.5s
Breakwater, south end Fl.WR.2s12m5M
Lighthouse Pier Iso.WG.4s11m9M
A directional 055° DirF.WRG.15m9M light, with a F.R.9m9M light leads into the harbour entrance

Supplies

Shops, post office, telephone, hotel, *Calor Gas.*

Communications

Harbour office at north side of Eglinton Basin, VHF Ch 12.

East side of Arran

Charts

2126 (1:75,000), *2220, 2221* (1:36,000), OS map *69*

Dangers and marks

A race extends for about 2 miles south and south-west of Pladda during out-going tides.

The east shore of Arran is generally clean beyond a cable from the shore, but for a mile northeast of Kildonan Point at the south end of the island several drying reefs extend 2 cables from the shore.

Pladda Island south of Arran is 19 metres high with a 29-metre white lighthouse.

Holy Island, on the east side of Arran, is 311 metres high with a white lighthouse 23 metres high near the shore on its east side.

Lights

Pladda lighthouse Fl(3)30s40m23M
Holy Island Inner light Fl.G.3s14m10M
Pillar Rock lighthouse Fl(2)20s38m25M

Pladda from east.

Anchorages

Pladda provides some shelter on its east side, close inshore north of the jetty, on sand and weed.

The channel between Pladda and Arran is obstructed by rocks, and tidal streams there run at over 3 knots.

Whiting Bay, a mile south of the south entrance to Lamlash Harbour, has a long stone slipway, and visitors' moorings north of it are usable in offshore winds.

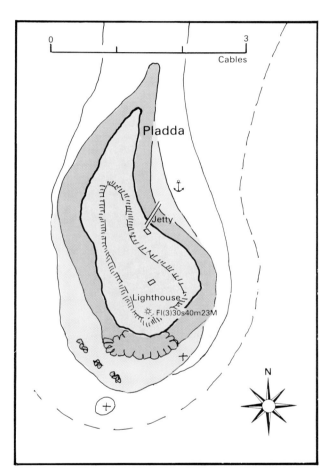

Pladda lighthouse from south.

Lamlash Harbour

55°32′N 5°06′W

Sheltered by Holy Island, this is the main anchorage on Arran, although possibly more suitable for a fleet of warships than a yacht. There are at least a dozen large ship moorings, painted yellow, but none of them lit. In northwest winds the bay is affected by violent squalls from the mountains. Easterly winds send some sea into the harbour, affecting even the anchorage at Holy Island.

Chart

Plan on *1864* (1:20,000), OS map *69*

Tides

Constant 0000 Greenock (+0115 Dover)

Height in metres

MHWS	MHWN	MTL	MLWN	MLWS
3·2	2·7	1·9	1·0	0·4

Approach

In the south entrance pass east of Fullarton Rock red can light buoy.

In the north entrance a red can light buoy in mid-channel marks a spit extending from the north shore which has a depth of 5 metres a cable north of the buoy, so the buoy can be passed on its north side by yachts in quiet conditions.

Lights

Holy Island Inner light, at the east side of the south entrance, Fl.G.3s14m10M, obscured from east of 147° and north of 282°

Fullarton Rock buoy Fl(2)R.12s

Buoy in north entrance Fl.R.6s

There are no navigation lights within the bay and it is difficult to see mooring buoys against the glare of street lights at night.

Anchorages

For ½ mile northeast and ¾ mile south of Lamlash Pier the shore dries for over ¼ mile. There are permanent moorings off Lamlash Pier and both moorings and fish cages north of Kingscross Point on the west side of the south entrance.

Depending on wind direction anchor clear of moorings north of Kingscross Point; or 4 cables west of Clauchlands Point at the north side of the north entrance; or clear of moorings east of Lamlash Pier.

In easterly winds anchor to the south of the house at the northwest end of Holy Island, clear of the mooring and slip. There are wrecks close inshore in front of the house. Landing on Holy Island is discouraged.

Lamlash Harbour from south. Holy Island Inner light in the foreground.

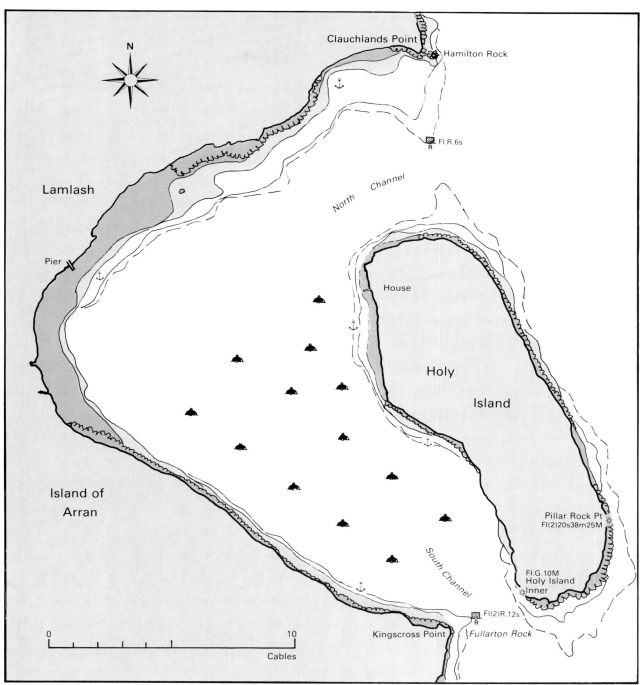

Lamlash

Supplies and services at Lamlash

Shops, post office, bank, telephone, hotel, *Calor Gas*, petrol, diesel, water, EC Wednesday. Chandlery and marine engineer ☎ Lamlash (07706) 333.

Brodick

55°35′N 5°09′W

The village is on the south side of the bay and Brodick Castle is on the northwest side. Two Admiralty buoys are moored in the bay. Fierce squalls are to be expected from the valley at the head of the bay in westerly winds.

Chart

Plan on *1864* (1:25,000), OS map *69*

Tides

Constant 0000 Greenock (+0115 Dover)

Height in metres

MHWS	MHWN	MTL	MLWN	MLWS
3·2	2·7	1·9	1·0	0·4

Anchorage and berths

There are suitable depths to anchor on the north-west side of the bay below Brodick Castle.

A tiny harbour is formed between the pier and a separate linkspan to the east of it on the south side of the bay, but this is completely shut in when a steamer is alongside. Yachts may be able to berth temporarily on the west face of the pier, but keep clear of the ferry berth; dues are charged.

Supplies

Shops, post office, telephone, hotel, *Calor Gas*. Moped and bicycle hire.

Lights

The Admiralty buoys are lit Fl.Y.2s and Fl.Y.4s
Brodick Pier head 2F.R(vert)9m4M

Firth of Clyde Channel

Chart

1907 (1:25,000)

Tides

South of Garroch Head, the south point of Bute, there are overfalls on the ebb tide.

Streams in the Firth of Clyde Channel run at 1 knot at springs and more over banks (causing turbulence, particularly with wind against tide), turning about 20 minutes before high and low water.

Constant at Millport is −0015 Greenock (+0100 Dover).

Height in metres

MHWS	MHWN	MTL	MLWN	MLWS
3·4	2·8	1·9	1·0	0·5

Dangers

The passage from Cumbrae to Cloch Point is generally clean outwith 1½ cables from the shore except for the dangers described below.

On the west shore a mile north of Toward Point a reef known as The Bridges extends 4 cables from the shore, marked by a red stone beacon, Innellan, inshore of its outer end.

Just over 5 miles NNE of Toward Point and 3 cables SSE of Dunoon Pier lies The Gantocks, a detached drying reef which is marked by a red light beacon at its southeast corner and a north cardinal buoy on its northwest side. The clear passage northwest of The Gantocks is 2 cables wide.

On the east shore, Lunderston Bay, 1¼ miles south of Cloch Point, dries out for nearly ¼ mile.

Ship channels

Ship channels which may be used by vessels constrained by their draught, are marked by buoys as follows:

Firth of Clyde Channel, marked by a total of five high focal plane buoys in the centre of the channel, spaced several miles apart.

Skelmorlie Channel, marked by lateral buoys branching eastwards from a point northwest of Great Cumbrae, for vessels of deeper draught than those which can use Firth of Clyde Channel.

Hunterston Channel, east of the Cumbraes, marked by lateral buoys. This is described on subsequent pages.

It is useful to know which channel large vessels are making for and for this purpose they show numeral pennant 1 for the Firth of Clyde Channel and pennant 2 for Skelmorlie Channel.

Marks

Cumbrae Elbow lighthouse, a white tower 11 metres in height, on the west side of Little Cumbrae.

Rubha'n Eun light beacon, a white metal tower 8 metres in height, on the southeast point of Bute.

Hunterston Nuclear Power Station, two blocks 63 metres and 70 metres high, on the mainland east of Little Cumbrae.

Ascog Patches pile beacon, 7 cables off the Bute shore 1¼ miles southeast of Bogany Point, black with two red bands and a topmark of two balls, is of no significance to yachts, but a useful reference point.

Toward Point lighthouse (accent on the first syllable of 'Toward'), a white tower 19 metres in height, at the north side of the entrance to Rothesay Sound with lattice radio masts north of the lighthouse.

Innellan Beacon, red with ball topmark, a mile north of Toward Point.

A large quarry on the west shore, 4 miles north of Toward Point, is a mile south of The Gantocks.

Inverkip Power Station chimney, 238 metres high, on the east shore, is the principal mark in this passage.

Cloch Point lighthouse, a low white stone tower with a black band 2½ miles north of Inverkip Power Station.

Lights

Many buoys in the Firth of Clyde Channel are lit but these are generally of no significance to yachts except insofar as they mark the deep-water channels. The principal lights are as follows:

Cumbrae Elbow lighthouse Fl.3s31m23M
Rubha'n Eun light beacon Fl.R.6s8m12M
Ascog Patches pile beacon Fl(2)10s5M
Toward Point lighthouse Fl.10s21m22M
The Gantocks Fl.R.2·5s12m18M
Cloch Point Fl.3s24m8M
Innellan beacon is not lit

Occasional anchorages on the east coast of Bute

Glencallum Bay, immediately southwest of Rubha'n
Eun lighthouse; only 1 cable wide, with a rock
drying 2·1 metres in the middle.

Kilchattan Bay, 1½ miles north of Rubha'n Eun.
The head of the bay dries for 3 cables and then
the bottom drops steeply. There is a narrow shelf
off the east end of Kilchattan village on the south
side of the bay, and a more extensive area ¼ mile
off the north side of the bay.

Hunterston Channel

Overfalls form off the south end of Little Cumbrae
which should be given a good berth particularly
with an ebb tide against a fresh southerly wind.
Fishing floats are laid up to ½ mile south of Little
Cumbrae.

On the east side of the channel, Hunterston
Sands, on which an oil rig building yard has been
built, dry out for a mile. Hunterston Ore and Coal
Loading Jetty, with large travelling cranes on its
head, extends 4 cables from the shore 1 mile NNE
of the oil rig yard.

Brigurd Spit extends up to 4 cables from the shore
south of the oil rig yard. South of Brigurd Spit the
outfall from Hunterston Power Station, which is
marked by a yellow conical light buoy, causes severe
turbulence.

Little Cumbrae

55°43′N 4°56′·5W

Little Cumbrae anchorage from southwest. Castle Island is in the
right foreground.

Anchorage on the east side of the island in the bay
between Castle Island, which has a ruined castle at
its north end, and Broad Island, 3 cables further
north. Drying reefs extend north and south of Trail
Isle, ½ cable east of Castle Island. The anchorage is
subject to a disturbing tidal swell.

A shoal lies 1 cable offshore ¼ mile southeast of
Sheanawally Point, the north end of Little Cumbrae, and a bank dries ½ cable northwest of the
point.

Landing on Little Cumbrae is forcefully discouraged as the island is actively maintained as a
nature reserve.

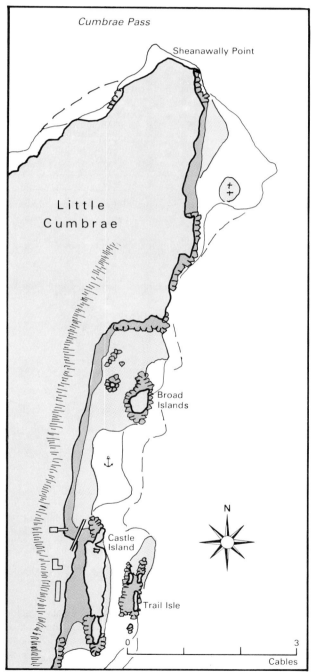

Little Cumbrae Island

Great Cumbrae

Millport

55°45′N 4°55′W

A small town at the south end of Great Cumbrae, built round a bay in which are two small islands (The Eileans) and a collection of rocks both above water and drying. In most of the bay east of The Eileans where depths are suitable for anchoring there are moorings.

Chart

Plan on *1867* (1:12,500)

Tides

Constant −0015 Greenock (+0100 Dover)

Height in metres

MHWS	MHWN	MTL	MLWN	MLWS
3·4	2·8	1·9	1·0	0·5

Approach and moorings

Approach the pier with its head showing between The Eileans and The Spoig rock 333°. The church tower in line with the pier head is on this bearing.

An alternative approach is along the shore from southwest inshore of The Clach and The Leug rocks, taking care to avoid the drying reef at Nupkur Point.

HIDB visitors' moorings have been laid SSE of the pier and there is also space to anchor southwest of the pier, clear of the moorings and rocks.

Plans are in hand to restore the pier and construct a wave screen on its north side to provide a berth for visiting yachts.

Lights

Leading lights 333° F.R.7/9m5M lead to the pier, but ferry services to Millport have been discontinued and these lights should not be relied on. Car ferries do sometimes berth overnight at Millport in easterly winds.

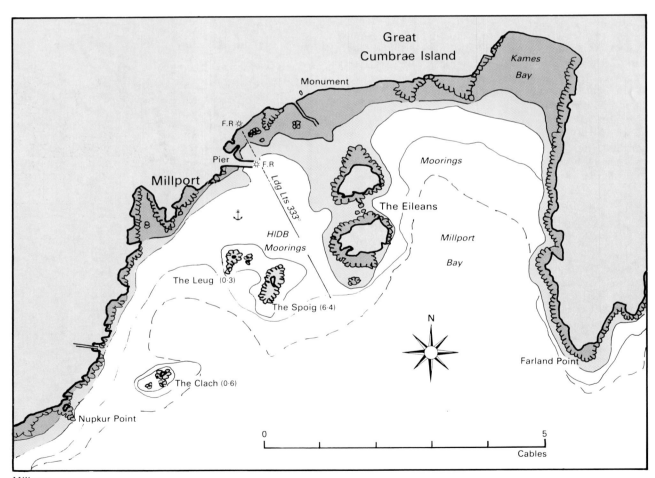

Millport

Millport from south-southeast, before the installation of visitors' pontoons. The Eileans are to the right with the pier at the top of the photo.

The back leading mark at Millport is in line with the church tower.

Supplies

Shops, post office, telephone, hotel, *Calor Gas*, petrol, diesel, water at pier, EC Wednesday.

Communications

Harbourmaster ☎ Largs (0475) 530826. Chandlery ☎ Largs (0475) 530806.

Largs Channel

Charts

Plan on *1867* (1:12,5000), *1907* (1:25,000)

Directions

Fairlie Roads, 55°45'·5N 4°52'W, 4·5 cables northeast of Hunterston Jetty head and 3 cables SSW of the NATO Pier provides occasional anchorage within ¼ mile northwest of the west cardinal perch at Fairlie Yacht Club slip. Fairlie Pier has been demolished. Since Largs Yacht Haven was opened fewer yachts are now moored at Fairlie, but there may be discarded tackle on the bottom. The foreshore dries off 1½ cables. An unlit mooring buoy, 3 cables SSW of the NATO Pier elbow, is a hazard if approaching by night.

Fairlie Patch, with a depth of 0·3m ¼ mile ENE of Hunterston Jetty head, is marked on its west side by a starboard-hand light buoy (recently moved from northwest of the rock).

Avoid obstructing access to any of the piers, and keep well clear of vessels manoeuvring.

Lights

There are no major lights but many lateral light buoys.

Hunterston Jetty 2F.G(vert) at both ends of its head, and it is lit up like a Christmas tree

NATO Pier 2F.G(vert) at both ends of its head

Largs Yacht Haven Oc.G.10s4m4M on the south side and Oc.R.10s4m4M on the north side of the entrance

Largs Pier 2F.G(vert)7m5M at its north end

Largs Yacht Haven

55°46'·5N 4°51'·5W

Tides

Constant −0005 Greenock (+0110 Dover)

Height in metres

MHWS	MHWN	MTL	MLWN	MLWS
3·4	2·8	1·9	1·0	0·5

Directions

Close north of the NATO Pier, the marina is accessible at all states of tide. The shore dries off south of the entrance to the end of the south breakwater, for about 50 metres on the outer side of the north breakwater, and the entrance channel is very narrow. Make for the RW entrance buoy before entering.

In easterlies strong winds are funnelled down Kelburn Glen, inland from the entrance.

Inside the marina shoal water on the south side is marked by small green spherical buoys, and an underwater obstruction east of the head of the north

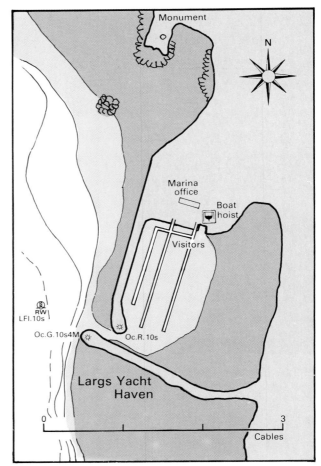

Largs Yacht Haven

breakwater by a small red buoy. The east shore of the marina dries for a cable, marked by small orange buoys. Visitors' berths are at the north end of the lane between the second and third row of pontoons.

Lights

At night the RW light buoy off the entrance is lit LFL.10s, and there is a light on the head of each breakwater, Oc.G.10s on the south side, Oc.R.10s on the north side, but they are difficult to pick out at night against shore lights and are sometimes extinguished. An Admiralty mooring buoy ¾ mile NNW of the entrance, and directly in the approach from that direction, is charted as lit but is reported to be extinguished.

Supplies

At Largs, 1½ miles, are shops, post office, telephone, hotel, petrol, EC Wednesday.

At marina are *Calor Gas,* diesel, water, chandlery.

Communications

Marina office VHF Ch M ☎ 675333. Slip, 45-ton hoist, repairs to hull, machinery and electrics.

Largs Marina from northwest. The water to the east of the pontoons is shoal; visitors' berths are at the inner end of a long corridor of pontoon berths.

Moorings

Ballochmartin Bay on the east side of Great Cumbrae is mostly occupied by small-craft moorings and an unlit mooring buoy is laid 3 cables SSE of the ferry slip. A clear passage must be left for access to the ferry slip.

Tomont End at the north end of Great Cumbrae has some boat moorings but may have space for anchoring.

Largs Pier

55°47'·7N 4°52'·3W

Temporary anchorage north or south of the pier, approximately east of the north end of Great Cumbrae, or at the pier itself, which has 2 metres alongside, but take care to avoid obstructing approach to the car ferry ramp inshore of the pier.

Lights

At night lights, 2F.G(vert), are shown at the north end of the pier, and an unlit mooring buoy is laid a cable north of the pier.

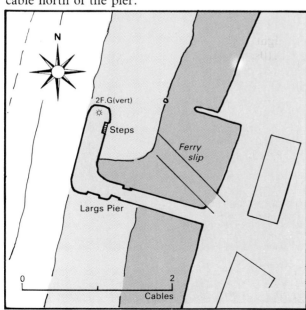

Largs Pier

Barrfields Slip

3 cables north of Largs Pier, is 12-metres wide and is suitable for launching trailer-sailers. The slip is also used by an RNLI inshore lifeboat for which space must be left at all times. No charge is made for the use of the slip, but launching a boat there would be an appropriate occasion to put a contribution in the RNLI collecting box.

Wemyss Bay Pier

55°52'·5N 4°53'·5W

Temporary anchorage north or south of the pier, leaving space for the Bute car ferry to manoeuvre at the pier. A new yellow pile structure with a cross topmark 4 cables NNW of the pier in a depth of 15 metres (lit Oc(2)Y.10s) is a convenient marker for the anchorage.

Anchorages on the west side of the Firth

Innellan, 55°54'N 4°57'W, temporary anchorage north or south of the old ferry jetty which is a mile north of Innellan Beacon.

Dunoon, 56°57'N 4°55'W, temporary anchorage a cable off a stone jetty (which dries) 1½ cables north of the main ferry pier, but you need to be a cable offshore to find a depth of 3 metres. West Bay, 3 cables southwest of the pier, is an alternative anchorage although more exposed to the south.

In approach, keep clear of The Gantocks, a detached drying reef 3 cables SSE of Dunoon Pier, marked by a red light beacon at its southeast corner and an unlit north cardinal buoy on its northwest side. The passage northwest of The Gantocks is 2 cables wide.

Shops, post office, telephone, hotel, *Calor Gas*, petrol and diesel at garages. Car ferry to Gourock.

Kip Marina approach from southwest. Inverkip Power Station
and jetty on the right.

Kip Marina from west.

Kip Marina approach channel is marked by pairs of small buoys.

Kip Marina

55°54'·5N 4°53'W

A marina formed from a gravel pit at the mouth of Kip Water, ½ mile north of Inverkip Power Station. It is entered through a dredged channel marked by pairs of buoys, with a nominal depth of over 2 metres, although it has been reported to have less. The entrance to the channel is marked by *Kip* G conical light buoy.

Lights

At night the power station jetty is marked by 2F.G(vert) lights at both ends, and *Kip* buoy has a faint Q.G light. If this buoy is not seen, approach keeping one walkway light at the pontoon on the southeast side in sight in the entrance.

Tides

Constant −0005 Greenock (+0110 Dover)

Height in metres

MHWS	MHWN	MTL	MLWN	MLWS
3·4	2·9	2·0	1·1	0·5

Supplies

Calor Gas, petrol, diesel, water, telephone. Shops, post office in village ½ mile. Hotel 200 metres.

Facilities

Showers, laundry, chandlery, 40-ton boat-hoist, repairs.

Communications

Marina office ☎ Largs (0475) 521485, VHF Ch M.

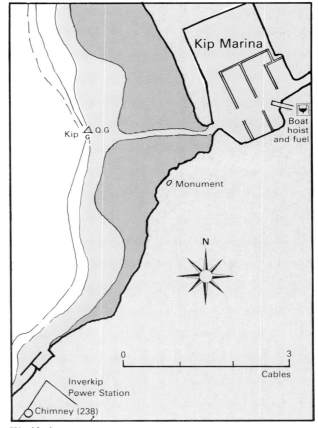

Kip Marina

III. Loch Long to River Clyde

The head of the Firth of Clyde consists of a basin north and east of Cloch Point, south of Loch Long, extending 7 miles from west to east with 3 lochs branching off it. The River Clyde enters from the east, south of Greenock Bank the west end of which is only two cables off Clydeport Container Terminal.

The anchorages and branch lochs are described in a clockwise sequence.

Rothesay Sound and the Kyles of Bute are covered in Chapter IV.

Chart

1994 (1:15,000) is essential for information about shipping channels and buoyage in this area.

Tides

Constant 0000 Greenock (+0115 Dover)

Height in metres

MHWS	MHWN	MTL	MLWN	MLWS
3·4	2·9	1·9	1·0	0·4

Restricted and prohibited areas

Holy Loch, Loch Long and Gareloch are Dockyard Ports, under the control of the Queen's Harbourmaster. Specific areas within these lochs are designated as prohibited areas from which all civilian craft are excluded at all times, and restricted and protected areas, within which no civilian craft

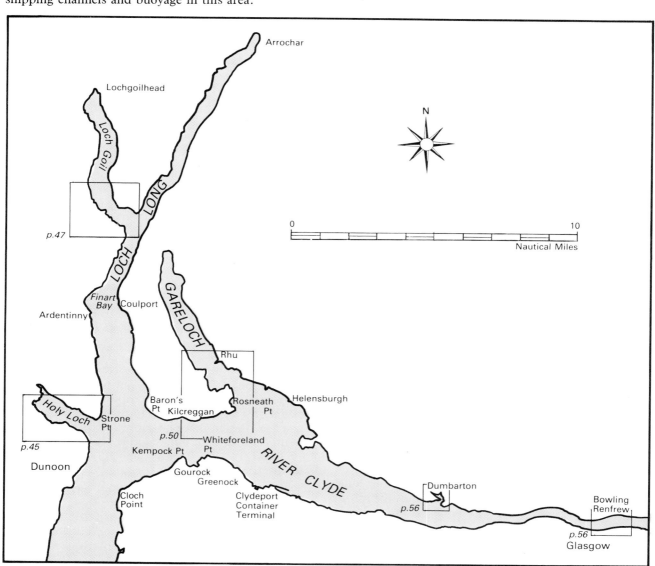

may enter or remain during the movement of nuclear submarines or large naval vessels. These are shown on the relevant plans.

When restricted/protected areas are closed to non-naval vessels signals are shown from naval establishments and escorting naval vessels in the area and are described where appropriate below. These areas leave space for small craft to continue on a passage without great difficulty, except possibly at Rhu Narrows.

Anchorages

Many Clyde anchorages consist of no more than an indentation in the shore of a loch, or sometimes only a length of shore where there are moderate depths and reasonable holding. Very often the shore dries for up to ¼ mile or, at the head of a loch, more than a mile, with a narrow shelf of moderate depth the edge of which drops suddenly into much deeper water.

It is often not practicable to describe the distance from the shore at which one should anchor; specific hazards are described, but otherwise it is necessary to check the depth while approaching.

By using a large-scale chart, many more occasional anchorages will be found than can be listed.

Marks

Rosneath Patch, ¾ mile north of Whiteforeland Point, on which is a lattice light beacon, is the main hazard in this area.

A lattice mast on Gallow Hill (Rosneath Point) on the north shore is conspicuous.

Ashton buoy, a safe-water buoy a mile WNW of Kempock Point, is a turning point in the Firth of Clyde Channel and an important reference point.

Kempock Point and Princes Pier at the west side of Gourock Bay are about 2½ miles ENE of Cloch Point.

Whiteforeland Point, with a conspicuous block of red brick buildings is ¾ mile east of Kempock Point.

Clydeport Container Terminal, with conspicuous blue cranes, is a mile ESE of Whiteforeland Point.

Deep-water channels

The Firth of Clyde Channel runs northeast to *Ashton* buoy, then east to *Whiteforeland* buoy, about 3 cables NNE of Whiteforeland Point, then ESE to Clydeport Container Terminal.

Loch Long Channel runs due north from Cloch Point.

Ardmore Channel branches ENE from Ashton buoy to pass north of Rosneath Patch and thence to Gareloch.

Kilcreggan Channel follows the north shore, between Loch Long and the Gareloch.

Note that the direction of buoyage changes at Baron's Point at the mouth of Loch Long, so that the starboard-hand light buoy *Kil No. 3* is on the northeast side of the channel.

It is essential for yachts to keep out of the way of vessels which can only use the deep-water channels, and a good lookout must be kept for them. Beware also car ferries, whose helmsmen may not be too scrupulous about the Collision Regulations.

Signal flags in the form of numeral pennants of the International Code are flown by ships to indicate which channel they are using, as follows:

1 Firth of Clyde Channel
2 Skelmorlie Channel
3 River Channel
4 Ardmore Channel
5 Loch Long Channel
6 Holy Loch
7 Kilcreggan Channel

Anchorages for large ships are designated north of *Ashton* buoy and east of Rosneath Patch. Ships leaving a channel for one of these anchorages fly First Substitute pennant of the International Code.

Lights

Many light buoys do not directly concern yachts, and these may be found on the chart; the principal lights are as follows:

Ashton buoy Iso.5s
Kempock Point beacon 2F.G(vert)10m3M
Whiteforeland buoy LFl.10s
Rosneath Patch beacon Fl(2)10s
Lateral buoys show Fl.R.2s (port hand) and Fl.G.5s (starboard hand)

Holy Loch

55°59′N 4°55′W

Charts

1994 (1:15,000), 3746 (1:25,000), OS map 63

Formerly one of the principal centres of British yachting, Holy Loch is now largely occupied by the US Navy, nominally based on floating installations in the middle of the loch, but gradually expanding ashore.

The head of the loch dries out for ½ mile and the shores on either side up to a cable. Submerged rocks extend 1½ cables south of Strone Point, the north point of the entrance to Holy Loch, marked by a south cardinal light buoy ¼ mile south of the point.

Restrictions

The whole loch is a Dockyard Port and the restrictions described at the beginning of this chapter apply. Two protected areas and a restricted area are established around the USN floating dock and headquarters ship in the middle of the loch, as shown on the plan.

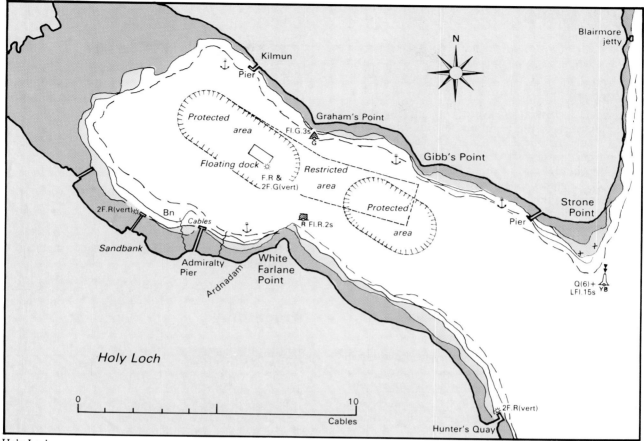

Holy Loch

Entry to the western protected area is prohibited at all times.

Entry to the eastern protected area is prohibited when the following signals are shown on the southeast corner of the floating dock: a red over two green lights vertically disposed and by day, a red flag with a white diagonal bar.

Entry to the restricted area is prohibited when the following signals are shown on the southeast corner of the floating dock: 3 F.G(vert) lights supplemented by signal flags International Code Pennant over Pennant 9.

Holy Loch is subject to violent squalls in strong westerly winds.

Tides

Constant 0000 Greenock (+0115 Dover)

Height in metres

MHWS	MHWN	MTL	MLWN	MLWS
3·4	2·9	1·9	1·0	0·4

Lights

Hunter's Quay ferry slip 2F.R(vert)6m6M
Strone Point light buoy Q(6)+LFl.15s
White Farlane Point light buoy Fl.R.2s
Graham's Point light buoy Fl.G.3s
Sandbank Pier 2F.R(vert)
F.R+2F.G(vert) at southeast corner of floating
  dock when eastern protected area is closed

Anchorages, south shore

Hunter's Quay, north but clear of the ferry slip, although there are several permanent moorings. Also between Hunter's Quay and White Farlane Point, but the shore dries up to a cable; some visitors' moorings are laid here by an hotel for the use of its customers.

Ardnadam, northwest of White Farlane Point; a cable area extends 1¼ cables east and ¾ cable west of Admiralty Pier.

Sandbank, as convenient, west of the cable area at Admiralty Pier. Supplies at Sandbank include shops, post office, telephone, hotel, water at Holy Loch SC close southeast of Sandbank Pier.

Anchorages, north shore

Strone, west of a stone pier about 2 cables west of Strone Point, the north point of the entrance.

Gibb's Point, to the west of the point, which is about 6 cables west of Strone Point.

Kilmun, about a cable northwest of a stone pier 3 cables northwest of Graham's Point. An underwater pipeline runs southwest from beacons on the shore about 70 metres northwest of the pier. Supplies at Kilmun include shops, post office, telephone, hotel, water at pier.

Loch Long

Chart

3746 (1:25,000), OS map *56*

Restrictions

The whole loch is a Dockyard Port and the restrictions described at the beginning of this chapter apply. At Coulport on the east shore about 5 miles from the entrance a prohibited area extends 150 metres from the shore, from about 7 cables south to a mile north of Coulport Jetty, and a restricted area extends most of the way across the loch from the jetty.

Finnart Oil Terminal, also on the east shore 1¼ miles northwest of the north point of the entrance to Loch Goil, is used by very large tankers which have to manoeuvre in a restricted space.

Glenmallan Jetty, a mile further northeast with conspicuous refuelling derricks, has a prohibited area extending 150 metres off it.

Dangers

Mountains fall steeply to the loch on both sides and there is no road along much of the west shore. Severe squalls can be expected from the mountains.

Overhead power lines cross Loch Long south of the entrance to Loch Goil with a clearance of 76 metres.

Tides

Constant −0005 Greenock (+0110 Dover)

Height in metres

MHWS	MHWN	MTL	MLWN	MLWS
3·4	2·9	2·0	0·9	0·3

Tidal streams throughout are negligible.

Marks

At the entrance *Loch Long* RW light buoy marks the centre of Loch Long Channel.

A new yellow pile beacon with an x topmark stands a cable SSW of Baron's Point at the east side of the entrance.

Coulport Jetty and Finnart Oil Terminal on the east shore, respectively 4 and 8 miles from the entrance, are conspicuous.

Lights

Loch Long light buoy (centre of the entrance) Oc.6s
Light buoy *Kil No. 3* off Baron's Point Fl.G.5s
Pile beacon *No. 3* off Baron's Point Oc(2)Y.10s3M
Ravenrock Point light beacon on the west shore 3 miles from the entrance, Fl.4s12m10M, has a directional light 204° showing NNE up the loch, with narrow F.WRG sectors and very narrow Al.WR and Al.WG sectors at the edges of the white sector
Coulport Jetty 2F.G(vert) at each end (with port closure signals)

Portdornaige light beacon on west shore Fl.6s8m11M
Construction jetty, 8 cables north of Coulport 2F.G(vert)9m5M
Dog Rock, at north side of Loch Goil entrance, Fl.2s7m11M
Finnart Oil Terminal has four sets of 2F.G(vert)

Anchorages

Cove Bay, on the east shore ¾ mile north of Baron's Point, the east point of the entrance to Loch Long; many small-craft moorings and a large unlit mooring buoy.

Blairmore, on the west shore, 3 cables north of ferry jetty. Shops, post office, telephone, hotel, EC Thursday.

Ardentinny

At the south point of Finart Bay which is 4 miles north of Strone Point on the west shore (not to be confused with Finnart, further north on the east shore).

The north side of the point is too deep for anchoring, but there are reasonable depths to the south. An uncharted rock lies close inshore below the houses on the south side of the bay. Visitors' moorings are provided by the hotel.

Other anchorages

Shepherd's Point Finart Bay dries out for 2 cables, dropping abruptly to 20 metres with a row of Admiralty moorings close to the LW line usually occupied by lighters, but there are reasonable depths east and northeast of a yellow beacon at the north end of the bay.

Loch Goil

The entrance is on the west side of Loch Long, between Rubha nan Eoin on the south side and Dog Rock, on which is a white light beacon, on the north side. An unlit mooring buoy lies ½ mile west of Dog Rock and a rock dries 1 metre ¾ cable from the shore inshore of the buoy, 2 cables east of Carraig na Maraig the next point on the north shore.

On the southwest shore, ½ mile northwest of Rubha nan Eoin, a drying spit extends a cable from the shore. 4 cables north of Carrick Castle on the west shore a submerged reef extending over 2 cables off the mouth of Carrick Burn, is marked by a beacon, which is on the shallowest part of the reef, not on its east edge.

Loch Goil is used for submarine trials and is sometimes closed to other vessels. Keep clear of Douglas Pier (a mile from the head of the loch on the west side), and Admiralty buoys and rafts.

Swine's Hole

Rubha Ardnahein is a low grassy spit on the southwest side of Loch Goil ¾ mile from Rubha nan Eoin with a drying spit, Roinn Diomhain, ¼ mile southeast of it; the bight between the two spits is a popular anchorage. The bay southeast of Roinn Diomhain is an alternative or overflow anchorage.

There is excellent walking in Queen Elizabeth Forest Park between Loch Goil and Ardentinny.

Carrick Castle

56°06′·5N 4°54′·5W

Tides

Constant −0005 Greenock (+0110 Dover)

Height in metres

MHWS	MHWN	MTL	MLWN	MLWS
3·3	2·8	1·8	0·9	0·3

Anchorage

Anchor either north or southeast of the castle, but the bottom is rocky in places and there are some boats on moorings.

Supplies

Shops, post office, telephone, hotel.

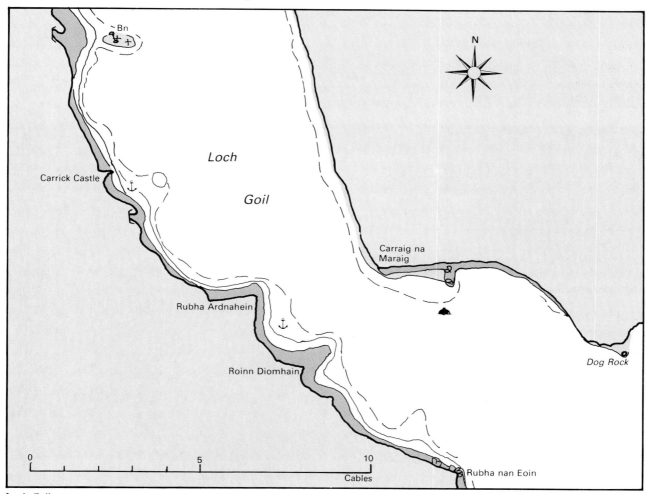

Loch Goil

Carrick Castle from south.

Lochgoilhead from south, showing the shoals at the river mouth.

Other anchorages

An alternative anchorage is 2 cables NNW of the perch off Carrick Burn which is 4 cables north of the castle. A note on the chart warns: 'Mariners are cautioned against anchoring between Leac Bhuidhe (½ mile north of the perch) and Blairlomond (north of Douglas Pier, about 3 miles north of the perch)', however there are moderate depths both north and south of the mouth of Cormonachan Burn, 8 cables north of the perch.

Keep clear of Douglas Pier and Admiralty mooring buoys and rafts.

Lochgoilhead, 56°10′N 4°54′W, any space suitable for anchoring is already occupied by moorings but, except at weekends, Loch Goil Cruisers usually have moorings available at their base south of Douglas Pier. Call at the office to confirm before leaving a boat on a mooring there even for a short visit ashore. Loch Goil Cruisers ☎ Lochgoilhead (030 13) 349/382. Supplies in Lochgoilhead include a small supermarket, restaurant, post office and telephone.

Upper Loch Long

Charts

3746 (1:25,000), 3740 (1:10,000)

The main features are Finnart Oil Terminal already described and Glenmallan Jetty on the southeast shore. On the northwest shore Cnap Point, ½ mile north of Finnart Oil Terminal, Ardgartan Point 1½ miles from the head of the loch, and the torpedo range buildings ¾ mile northeast of Ardgartan, are conspicuous. An obelisk stands 6 cables north of Cnap Point.

Ardgartan Point has a caravan site on it; the shore dries off for a cable southeast of the point, marked by a perch ESE of the point. The bight north of the point is occupied by moorings (and is very deep). There is a small area suitable for anchoring south of Ardgartan Point, east of a jetty and two beacons on the shore; also along a narrow strip between Ardgartan and the torpedo range buildings, but a main road runs along the shore here.

Arrochar

56°12′N 5°45′W

On the east shore anchor in a small bight north of Ardmay Hotel east of Ardgartan, a mile southwest of Arrochar; or between 4 cables southwest and a cable north of the church, or within 1½ cables north of the ruined pier; however the foreshore dries up to ½ cable and there is only a width of ¼ cable from the LW line with a depth of less than 10 metres.

Supplies

Shops, post office, telephone, hotel, *Calor Gas*, petrol and diesel at garage at the north end of village.

Occasional anchorage between Loch Long and Gareloch

Kilcreggan, 55°59′N 4°49′W, east of the pier at the east end of the village; disturbed by passing traffic afloat. Supplies include licensed grocer, post office, telephone, hotel, petrol.

Gareloch

Chart

2000 (1:10,000)

Restrictions

The whole loch is a Dockyard Port and a passage 1 cable wide in the approach to Rhu Narrows is a protected channel. Entry to the protected channel is prohibited when a red over two green lights vertically disposed together with, by day, a red flag with a white diagonal bar is shown at the following places: Faslane Floating Dock; RCT Port Unit, Rhu; Green Island, 2 cables north of Rosneath Point; navy buildings, Greenock; or naval auxiliary craft in the area. Except perhaps at Rhu Narrows there is plenty of space to sail outwith the protected channel.

Gareloch is home to many hundreds of yachts but there is now little to attract a visitor. The eastern shore is largely built up with naval installations, and suburban housing developments filling in the spaces between the Victorian houses. Even the site of McGruer's old yard on the west side is now a housing development.

Tides

Constant −0005 Greenock (+0110 Dover)

Height in metres

MHWS	MHWN	MTL	MLWN	MLWS
3·4	2·9	1·8	0·9	0·3

Dangers and marks

Perch Rock, an isolated drying rock 1¼ cables east of Green Island which is 1½ cables north of Rosneath Point at the southwest side of the entrance, is marked by a small yellow buoy close to its east side. A red light buoy (*No. 24*) lies over a cable ESE of the rock.

The bay northwest of Perch Rock dries, and the shore further north dries out 1 cable.

The shore on the northeast side of the entrance at Cairndhu Point dries out 2 cables.

The northeast side of the channel is marked by green light buoys and a light beacon.

At Rhu Narrows there are two red can light buoys on the west side of the channel.

The conspicuous buildings of the Royal Corps of Transport Port Unit are 4 cables NNW of Cairndhu Point. Rhu Marina is 2 cables west of the Port Unit.

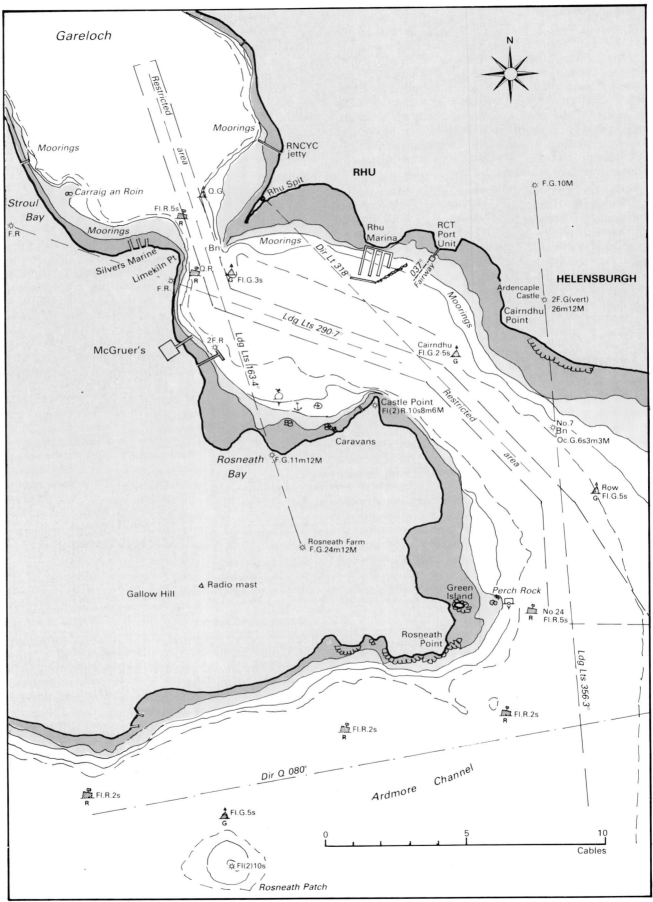

Gareloch

Moorings

Moorings

RNCYC
jetty

RHU

☀ F.G.10M

Stroul
Bay

Restricted   area

∞ Carraig an Roin

Rhu Spit

Rhu
Marina

RCT
Port
Unit

☀ F.R

Moorings

Fl.R.5s
R

Moorings

Bn

Q.G

Dir Lt 318°

037°
Fairway

HELENSBURGH

Silvers Marine

Limekiln Pt

Q.R
R

Moorings

G Fl.G.3s

Ardencaple
Castle

2F.G(vert)
26m12M

☀ F.R

Ldg Lts 290.7°

Moorings

Cairndhu
Point

McGruer's

2F.R

Ldg Lts 163.4°

Cairndhu
Fl.G.2·5s
G

⚓ ⊕

Castle Point
Fl(2)R.10s8m6M

Restricted

No.7
Bn
Oc.G.6s3m3M

Caravans

Rosneath
Bay

☀ F.G.11m12M

area

Row
G Fl.G.5s

Rosneath Farm
☀ F.G.24m12M

Gallow Hill

△ Radio mast

Green
Island

Perch Rock

Y

No.24
R Fl.R.5s

Rosneath
Point

Ldg Lts 356.3°

Fl.R.2s
R

Fl.R.2s
R

Fl.R.2s
R

Dir Q 080°

Ardmore   Channel

Fl.G.5s
G

0   5   10

Cables

☀ Fl(2)10s

Rosneath Patch

Gareloch approach from southwest. Castle Point, Rosneath, is in the right foreground. Rhu Marina is in the middle of the far shore, with Rhu Spit to the left and the RCT Port Unit to the right.

Rhu Narrows from south.

Rhu Spit, a further ½ mile west, dries over halfway across the narrows from the northeast shore; a white cylindrical beacon with a green band stands at its southwest end.

North of the narrows, the moorings of the Royal Northern and Clyde Yacht Club are on the east side, and Stroul Bay and many other yacht moorings on the west side.

Approach

Pass east of *No. 24* light buoy unless Perch Rock is clearly seen, and keep a good lookout for naval vessels. Keep to the side of the channel but take care not to wander into shoal water; make sure to pass west of Rhu Spit beacon if going beyond Rhu Narrows.

At Faslane Base, 2½–3 miles north of the narrows on the east shore, a prohibited area from which all craft are excluded extends 150 metres from the piers and floating dock. A restricted area extends from 56°03′N to 56°04′N across the loch from the east shore leaving a passage 1–2 cables wide along the west shore.

Entry to the restricted area at Faslane is prohibited when the following signals are shown on the floating dock: 3F.G(vert) lights supplemented by signal flags International Code Pennant over Pennant 9.

Lights

At night a wealth of leading lights are provided as follows, together with lateral light buoys.

Beacon No. 1 is a directional light beacon southeast of the entrance leading 080° through Ardmore Channel DirQ.WRG+VQ(4)Y.5s
No. 24 light buoy Fl.R.5s
Row light buoy Fl.G.5s
Ardencaple Castle leading lights 356·3°:
   Front Bn No. 7N Oc.G.6s3m3M
   Centre 2F.G(vert)26m12M
   Rear F.G.10M (822 metres from centre)
Cairndhu light buoy Fl.G.2·5s
Castle Point light beacon Fl(2)R.10s8m6M
Rosneath directional Lt 290·7° DirOc.WRG.3s14M
   Leading lights 290·7° F.R
Rosneath Bay leading lights 163·4°:
   Front F.G.11m12M
   Rear F.G.24m12M
Rhu Point Q(3)WRG.6s9m10·7M
   Directional Lt 318° DirOc.WRG.6s5m14M
Rhu Spit light beacon Fl.2·5s
Light buoy south of Rhu Spit Fl.G.3s
Light buoy southwest of Rhu Spit Q.R
Light buoy northwest of Rhu Spit Fl.R.5s
Light buoy north of Rhu Spit Q.G
Mambeg directional light 330° Q(4)WRG.8s

Keep a lookout at night for other traffic and for signal lights particularly at Green Island and the RCT Port Unit. It is best to keep off the leading lines.

Anchorages

Rosneath Bay, anchor not more than ½ cable ESE of a yellow spherical buoy with a cross topmark which is moored north of the front leading beacon on the shore. Drying rocks extend over a cable from the shore.

McGruer's yacht yard is on the west side of Rosneath Bay: ☎ (0436) 831313; slipping and all repairs.

Rhu Bay, between Cairndhu Point and Rhu Marina, dries up to 1½ cables from the shore and most available space is taken up with moorings. A fairway must be left to the RCT Port Unit, in line with the jetty there 037°. At night leading lights F.G are shown on this line.

Rhu Marina

The marina is entered at the southwest corner of Rhu Bay. The outer end of the breakwater covers and a strong tide runs across the entrance.

Services

Diesel, water, chandlery, *Calor Gas*.

Communications

Rhu Marina ☎ Rhu (0436) 820238, 820652 VHF Ch M (office hours).

Supplies

Shop, post office, telephone, hotel, in Rhu; more in Helensburgh, 1½ miles.

Other anchorages

Stroul Bay Carraig an Roinn approximately 4½ cables WNW from Limekiln Point at the west side of Rhu Narrows dries 3·0 metres, marked by a stout perch at its east side; an inviting-looking space there is not a suitable place to anchor.

Silvers' Marine on the south side of the bay provides moorings, showers, water, slipping and repairs. ☎ Rhu (0436) 831222.

Stroul Bay Yacht Haven provides moorings, showers, water, and diesel, ☎ Rhu (0436) 831430.

Nicholson Hughes Sailmakers are at Silvers' yard ☎ Rhu (0436) 831356.

Clynder Moorings extend 1½ miles along the west shore. Modern Charters, ☎ Rhu (0436) 831312, provide moorings and chandlery.

Royal Northern and Clyde Yacht Club moorings occupy the area north of Rhu Spit, and most of the east shore not occupied by the navy is full of permanent moorings.

Garelochhead The head of the loch dries for 1½ cables and most of the water with moderate depths is taken up by permanent moorings. Supplies in village.

Gourock Bay from east.

Helensburgh

56°00′N 4°44′W

A mile east of Gareloch entrance. The shore dries out 1½ cables almost to the head of Helensburgh Pier, and the 2-metre line is 1–2 cables further out. Temporary anchorage clear of the approach to the pier, which is used by excursion steamers. Temporary berth at side of the pier when rise of tide is sufficient. Supplies in town.

Gourock Bay

55°58′N 4°49′W

The west side of the bay is taken up by ferry quays and small-craft moorings, and the bottom between the quays and the moorings is foul. On the south side of the bay is a naval jetty, and a passage ½ cable wide is reserved in which anchoring is prohibited; the east side of the outer end of this passage is marked by a yellow light buoy. The east side of the bay dries off for a cable.

To use a mooring enquire at the boatyard. Land at the slip east of naval jetty.

Services

Boatyard, James Adam and Sons ☎ Gourock (0475) 31346. Moorings, Ritchie Bros ☎ Gourock (0475) 32125. Mackenzie Sailmakers ☎ Gourock (0475) 36196.

River Clyde

Charts

1994 is needed to beyond Great Harbour, 4°43′W. *2007* (1:15,000), OS map *63, 64*.

Tides

Port Glasgow

Constant is +0010 Greenock (+0125 Dover)

Height in metres

MHWS	MHWN	MTL	MLWN	MLWS
3·6	3·0	2·0	1·0	0·4

Glasgow

Constant is +0020 Greenock (+0135 Dover)

Height in metres

MHWS	MHWN	MTL	MLWN	MLWS
4·7	4·1	2·8	1·6	0·8

Tidal streams turn at about local HW and LW. Rates are not strong but out-going streams are increased and in-going streams reduced by heavy rain or melting snow; the out-going stream is enough to raise an unpleasant sea against a fresh westerly wind.

Requirements

Clyde Port Authority requires all small craft intending to go east of Clydeport Container Terminal to contact Estuary Control by telephone or VHF Ch 12 or 14, 12 hours beforehand.

Clydeport Container Terminal.

Passage east of a line between Rothesay Dock entrance (13 miles upriver from the Container Terminal) is not permitted for small craft except for the purpose of proceeding to or from a laying-up yard at Renfrew, and the skipper must be in possession of a permit, obtained from CPA, 16 Robertson Street, Glasgow G2, ☎ 041-221 8733.

Directions

The River Clyde is entered at Clydeport Container Terminal on the south shore and for the first 3 miles the channel closely follows the shore. The river is navigable for about 16 miles from Greenock but there is at present little to attract a yacht to enter it apart from various laying-up yards. However with the decline in commercial traffic, and extensive riverside development now in progress, Glasgow Harbour may become an attractive destination.

Custom House Quay, which is at the centre of a large-scale waterfront redevelopment in Greenock, is ½ mile southeast of the Container Terminal, after which the channel makes a double bend to starboard passing the embankment of the Great Harbour. A mile beyond the east end of Great Harbour the channel begins to leave the south shore and particular care must be taken for the next 4 miles to keep within the buoyed channel. At high water the estuary is over a mile wide here but the buoyed channel is less than a cable.

Dumbarton Castle on the north side of the river stands on a mound of rock 72 metres high. For the next two miles the south side of the channel is bounded by a stone training wall, the Lang Wark, a survival from the original 18th-century improvement works, which is submerged except at LWS but marked by stone beacons.

By the east end of the Lang Wark the channel has been reduced to the character of an inland river although still with a drying foreshore on the south side. At Dunglass on the north shore is a coastal tanker terminal and a mile further east is Bowling Harbour, obstructed by several sunken vessels, but used by some small craft.

Bowling Basin, the end of the abandoned Forth and Clyde Canal, which is entered through a lock from the east end of Bowling Harbour, is also used for berthing small craft, ☎ 041-332 6936. British Waterways Board has long-term plans for improving the basin; an inland section of the canal is being refurbished for pleasure craft, and there is some hope of its whole length eventually being reopened.

After a further mile the river is crossed by Erskine Bridge (headroom 52 metres) and for a further 3 miles the south bank is not very built-up. The River Cart joins the Clyde on the south side 2½ miles from Erskine Bridge and Rothesay Dock opens on the north side.

Passage notes

The Container Terminal has three large blue cranes which are easily seen from Gareloch entrance. If coming from Gareloch steer for the west end of the Container Terminal and pass west of *No. 2* red can light buoy.

Keep strictly to the buoyed channel as in some places there are stone banks very close outwith the channel. Keep to the starboard side whenever meeting another vessel.

As large vessels are only able to move near high water and have to keep to the dredged channel which is much narrower than the buoyed channel, the period around high tide should be avoided.

On a passage down river a lightly powered boat of less than about 10 metres will be hard pressed in a fresh westerly wind; in these conditions it may be better to make the passage at low water on the first of the flood when the water will be smoother.

Dumbarton

55°56′N 4°34′W

At the mouth of the River Leven on the north side of the river, 7 miles upriver from the Container Terminal. Leven Perch is a stone beacon ¼ mile southwest of Dumbarton Rock at the east side of the entrance, which is marked by miniature lateral buoys of which the first is ¼ cable northwest of Leven Perch.

The charted depth in the entrance is 2·4 metres, but where the channel bends to the west there is much less and it should be approached on a rising tide. McAlister's yard has pontoons in the river, with depths of little more than 1 metre alongside the outer pontoon, but the bottom is soft mud. The yard lays up yachts, carries out repairs, and supplies fuel, water and chandlery; ☎ Dumbarton (0389) 31500.

Services

Laying-up yards at Renfrew are: Clyde River Boat Yard, ☎ Glasgow 041-886 5974, and Marine Services Scotland, ☎ Glasgow 041-886 5469.

Marine Services have a boat-hoist at a dock on the south side of the river, 4 cables upstream from the mouth of the River Cart, with pontoons for waiting alongside. Passing vessels may cause a heavy surge in the dock.

Clyde River Boat Yard has a slip for its boat-hoist 9 cables upstream from the River Cart, about 1½ cables upstream from Renfrew Harbour which is close to Renfrew Ferry. There is nowhere to lie to wait for the boat-hoist nearer than Renfrew Harbour, apart from a massive piled jetty at a ship repair yard immediately downstream from the slip. Communication with the yard is best made by dinghy.

River Leven from Dumbarton Castle. Sandpoint, just left of centre, must be given a wide berth before turning towards the pontoons which are beyond the boatyard sheds at the left.

Dumbarton from southwest. Leven Perch, which is a substantial stone beacon, is in front of Dumbarton Rock at the right. The buoy to the left of Leven Perch must be left to port before turning in to the river.

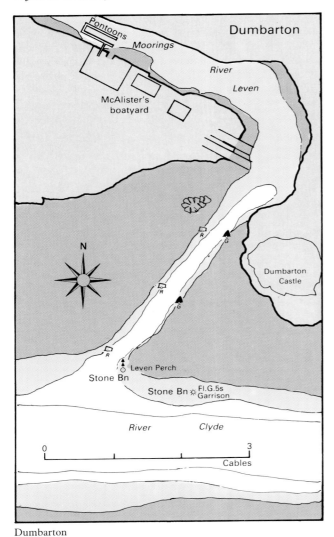

Dumbarton

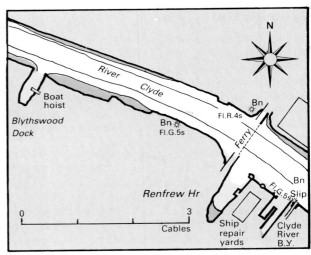

Renfrew Harbour

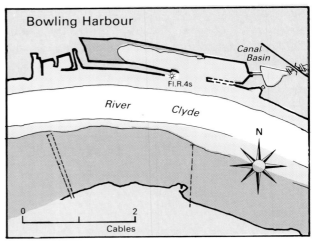

Bowling Harbour

River Clyde, looking upstream from Dumbarton Castle. The oil tanker berths at Dunglass are on the left, and the far side of the channel is marked by the Lang Wark, an 18th-century training wall.

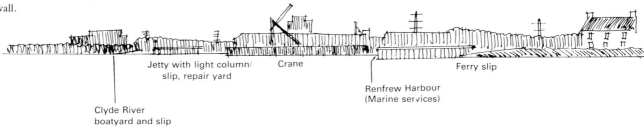

Renfrew from north.

IV. Kyles of Bute and Loch Fyne

The sequence of this chapter is from Rothesay Bay through the East Kyle to the Burnt Islands and Loch Riddon, continuing by the West Kyle to the West side of Bute, followed by Loch Fyne and the Crinan Canal.

Charts

2131 (1:75,000). Kyles: *1906* (1:25,000); *2383* (1:25,000) and *2221* (1:36,000) cover the west side of Bute. Chart *1907* (1:25,000) is needed at Toward Point.

Tidal streams

The flood tide enters both Kyles from seaward and the streams meet around the Burnt Islands; the actual point of meeting depends on meteorological conditions, but is normally a few miles east of the islands. The tidal stream in the passages at Rubha Ban and the Burnt Islands may reach 3 knots with the flood usually running eastward.

Buoyage

Direction of buoyage in Rothesay Sound and Loch Striven is towards northwest and north; in the West Kyle it is towards north and in the East Kyle southeast, changing at Ardmaleish Point, which has a north cardinal buoy on its north side.

Rothesay Sound and approaches to East Kyle

55°51′N 5°03′W

Chart

1907 (1:25,000), plan *1867* (1:10,000), OS map *63*

Tides

Constant −0015 (+0100 Dover)

Height in metres

MHWS	MHWN	MTL	MLWN	MLWS
3·6	3·1	2·1	1·2	0·6

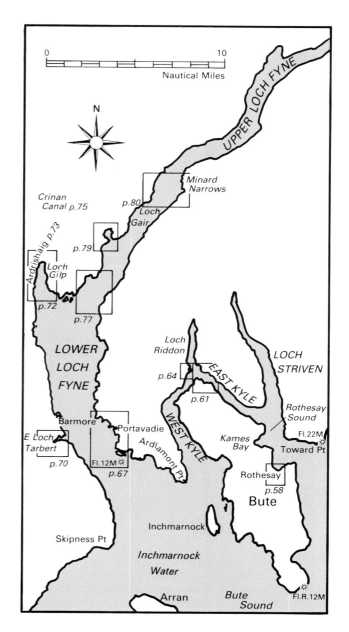

Dangers and marks

Toward Point lighthouse on the north side of the entrance to Rothesay Sound from the Firth of Clyde is a white tower 19 metres high, with a lattice tower behind it and two more lattice towers on the hillside further inland.

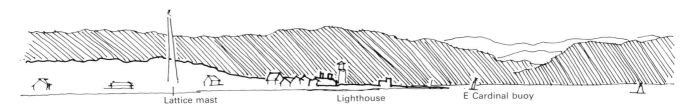

Toward Point from southwest.

At Toward Point a perch 1 cable south of the lighthouse stands on the end of a drying reef and *No. 34* east cardinal buoy is close southeast of a submerged reef which extends over ¼ mile SSW of the lighthouse. *No. 35* green conical light buoy marks Toward Bank with a least depth of 4·3 metres. Unmarked shoals and drying rocks extend two cables from the north shore between Toward and Ardyne.

The approach from seaward is straightforward but if coming from or going to the upper reaches of the firth, keep south of both the perch at Toward Point and *No. 34* east cardinal buoy.

Yellow light buoys around Ardyne Point are of no significance to yachts.

A stranger might mistake Loch Striven for the East Kyle, but the compass will soon clarify which is which. A boatyard stands on Ardmaleish Point which separates the East Kyle from Kames Bay.

Rothesay Bay

55°51′N 5°03′W

The bay is generally clean but there are several large mooring buoys (at present 3 of them). Rothesay Harbour is at the south side of the bay.

Lights

The most southwesterly of the mooring buoys is lit Fl.Y.2s.
Lights at Rothesay Harbour are 2F.R(vert) at the west end of Front Pier, 2F.G(vert) at the east end of Front Pier, and 2F.R(vert) on Albert Pier on the east side of the entrance to the Outer Harbour. These lights are all difficult to pick out against town lights.

Anchorages

The usual anchorage is off the west side of the bay, where there is a low rectangular building (Kyles of Bute Sailing Club) between the road and the water with a wood behind. Check the depth as it is shoal close inshore and the bottom falls away steeply a cable from the shore. Water from a tap below the clubhouse.

Space may be available in the Outer Harbour, of which the south half dries, or in the Inner Harbour, most of which dries, or on the south side of the west end of Front Pier, but keep close to Front Pier as the south shore dries.

In winds between north and east there is better shelter in Achavoulin Bay on the north side of Rothesay Sound, southwest of the Toward Sailing Club's stone pier.

Supplies and services

Shops, post office, bank, phone, hotels, chandlers, *Calor Gas*, swimming baths. EC Wednesday.
Diesel (minimum 200 gallons) and water at pier. Petrol, diesel in town. Repairs, see Port Bannatyne. Ferry to mainland.

Communications

Harbourmaster ☎ Rothesay (0700) 3842, VHF Ch 16, 12 (0600–2100).

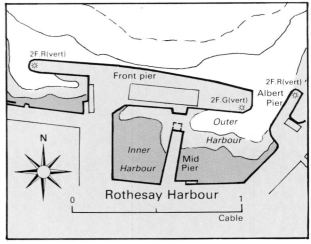

Rothesay

Kames Bay (Port Bannatyne)

55°52′N 5°04′W

The shores of the bay are drying or shoal up to 2 cables on all sides; in particular rocks dry out a cable NNE of Ardbeg Point at the south side of the bay, and it is shoal 1½ cables north of this point. There are several large Admiralty mooring buoys in the middle of the bay and many small-craft moorings.

Port Bannatyne from north.

Anchorage

Anchoring is prohibited near a small foul area 2 cables north of the boatyard slip (in any case the depth is about 20 metres). If space can be found anchor between the old pier and the boatyard slip, but the bottom falls away steeply; alternatively well off the northwest side of the bay; the shore dries out up to a cable but there is a shelf with reasonable depths.

Lights

There are no navigational lights.

Supplies and services

Shops, post office, phone, hotels. Water and *Calor Gas* at boatyard. Boatyards: Peter Macintyre (Clyde) Ltd and Ardmaleish Boat Building Co., ☎ Rothesay (0700) 2007.

Loch Striven

55°57′N 5°05′W

A bleak and rather featureless loch, notorious for squalls, running north for over six miles from the entrance to the East Kyle. Submarine exercises and experimental operations are sometimes carried out, and tankers are laid up in the upper parts of the loch.

Anchorages

There are only the most tenuous of anchorages, of which one is at Inverchaolain, northwest of a slight promontory at the mouth of a glen 2 miles north of the NATO fuel jetty on the east side of the loch; the bottom falls away very steeply.

The least insecure anchorage is at the head of the loch on the east side, ¼ mile from the head. Other berths may be found north of the point 3 cables further south, but much of the bight there dries out. A large yacht has a mooring there.

Anchorage at the head of Loch Striven. The yacht is on a permanent mooring.

East Kyle and the Burnt Islands

Tides

Constant −0015 Greenock (+0100 Dover)

Height in metres

MHWS	MHWN	MTL	MLWN	MLWS
3·2	2·8	2·0	1·2	0·6

Dangers and marks

The East Kyle is clean outwith a cable from the shore as far as Colintraive Point where there is an extensive drying area in the bight southeast of the point. Because of the hills close on each side, the Kyles can be very squally. Very strong squalls may be funnelled down Loch Striven and take a yacht by surprise which has thus far survived a passage from west to east.

At Rubha a'Bhodaich (Rhubodach) on the southwest shore a green conical buoy marks the end of a drying bank off the point.

Directions

There is a choice of two passages at the Burnt Islands. The passage north of Eilean Mor is narrower but briefer; the tide may be less strong in the southern passage.

In the northern passage the most conspicuous mark is a red beacon but the north side of the channel is defined by *No. 42* red can light buoy. There is only 50 metres distance between the red light buoy and the unlit green conical buoy SSW of it. At the northwest end of the passage a shoal extends west from Eilean Buidhe to within 50 metres of the northwest green conical light buoy.

Pass south of the red buoy and northeast of the two green buoys, and keep at least ½ cable off the north end of Eilean Fraoich. Tidal streams in both directions tend to set south from Eilean Buidhe.

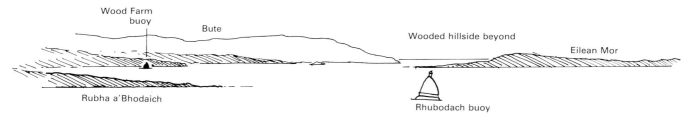

Burnt Islands south channel from east.

Burnt Islands from northwest. Rubha na Moine in left foreground.

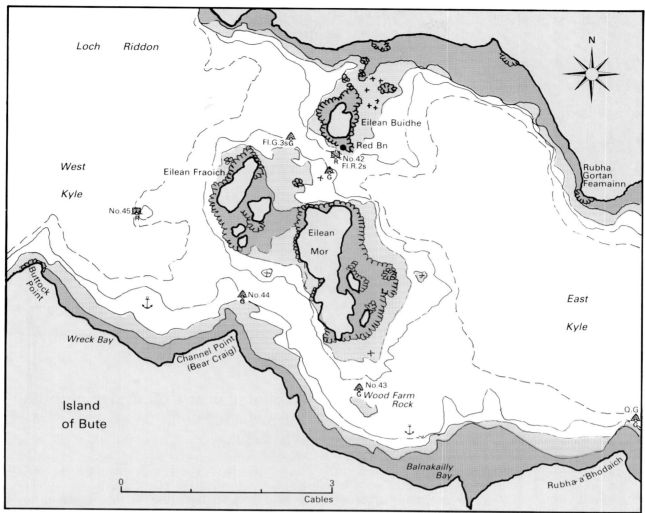

Burnt Islands

Burnt Islands south channel from west. Buttock Point and
Wreck Bay in the right foreground.

Burnt Islands north channel from southeast.

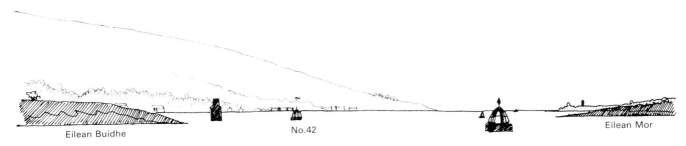

Burnt Islands north channel from northwest.

In the south passage shoals and drying rocks extend deceptively far south and southeast from Eilean Mor. Pass close north of Wood Farm Rock green conical buoy (*No. 43*).

Pass north of *No. 44* green conical buoy ½ cable north of Bear Craig (Channel Point); note that there is a depth of less than 1 metre ¼ cable southeast of the buoy. At LW springs beware also a rock ½ cable northeast of the buoy with a depth of 1·2 metres.

No. 45 red can buoy marks a rock with a least depth of 2·4 metres.

Lights

Rhubodach buoy is lit Q.G
In the north passage *No. 42* red buoy is lit Fl.R.2s and the northwest green buoy is lit Fl.G.3s

At night

To be sure of avoiding the reefs at the north end of Eilean Fraoich do not turn south into the West Kyle until Rubha Ban buoy Fl.R.4s shows open of the Buttock of Bute. Coming from the West Kyle keep Rubha Ban buoy in sight until the two light buoys in the north channel are in line.

Anchorages at Colintraive and the Burnt Islands

55°55'·5N 5°10'W

Southeast of Colintraive Point the shore dries off for 1½ cables. Here and further southeast the bottom falls away sharply. The best anchorage at Colintraive is west of the point, clear of cables and the ferry mooring and leaving space for the ferry to manoeuvre.

Supplies

Shop, post office, phone, hotel, water at the ferry slip.

Anchorages

Balnakailly Bay, south of Eilean Mor and clear of Wood Farm Rock.

Wreck Bay, between Channel Point (Bear Craig) and Buttock of Bute.

In westerly winds, some shelter may be found on the east sides of Eilean Mor or Eilean Buidhe.

Caladh Harbour

55°56′N 5°12′W

A small bay on the west shore ¾ mile WNW of the Burnt Islands sheltered from east by Eilean Dubh which is overgrown with rhododendrons, as is the hillside behind.

A stone beacon in the form of a miniature lighthouse stands on the west side of the south entrance and there are submerged rocks on both sides.

In the middle of the northeast entrance a rock above water is marked by a white stone beacon with a diamond topmark. A detached drying rock north of the beacon is sometimes marked by a perch, but if it is missing the beacon in the north entrance in line with the beacon at the south entrance clears it. Any part of a house at the north end of the bay in sight clears the south side of the drying rock.

Anchorage

The west side of the bay dries for about half its width, but twin-keel boats could dry out there. The island shore has some submerged and drying rocks close inshore, and a ring is fixed in the face of the stone cliff. This anchorage is often very crowded.

Caladh Harbour from southwest.

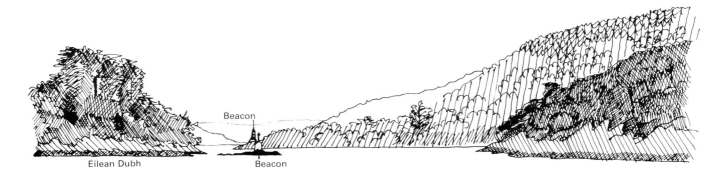

Caladh Harbour north entrance. The stone beacon in line with the stone beacon at the south end clears the drying rock north of the entrance.

Caladh Harbour North entrance. The first house on the right just showing clears the south end of the drying rock.

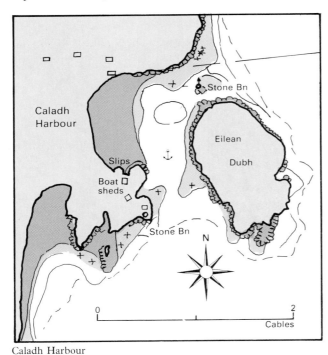

Caladh Harbour

Loch Riddon

The head of Loch Riddon dries for 1½ miles and the bottom drops away steeply almost everywhere. Most places suitable for anchoring are already occupied by permanent moorings, one of which might be available subject to the usual courtesies.

Anchorages

Ormidale, close north of the pier on the west shore, 1¼ miles north of Eilean Dubh at Caladh. The LW line is 2 cables north of the pier and most of the intervening space is taken up with moorings. Fish cages are moored to the south of the pier.

Salthouse, on the east shore ½ mile ENE of Ormidale pier, but the LW line extends across the loch from Salthouse.

Eilean Dearg, traditionally known as One Tree Island although it has now sprouted three rather half-hearted trees, off the east shore ¾ mile north of Eilean Dubh; there are moderate depths between the island and the shore, but beware a drying patch ½ cable north of the island.

Eilean Dearg from the west shore of Loch Riddon.

Ormidale. A puffer is alongside the stone quay. Yacht moorings to the right.

West Kyle

Tides

Constant −0015 Greenock (+0100 Dover)

Height in metres

MHWS	MHWN	MTL	MLWN	MLWS
3·4	3·1	2·2	1·4	0·9

Dangers and marks

At Rubha Ban on the northwest shore a mile southwest of the Buttock of Bute a red light buoy marks a drying spit on its northwest side. Half a mile north of Rubha Ban fish cages are marked by yellow light buoys.

From Rubha Ban the villages of Tighnabruaich and Kames stretch for 2½ miles along the northwest and west side of the Kyle, each with a pier and many boats on moorings and HIDB visitors' moorings.

South of Kames there are shoals and drying rocks up to 2 cables off the west shore, and up to 1 cable off the east shore; otherwise the Kyle is clean.

2½ miles south of Kames Pier, Carry Rock light buoy (*No. 46*) marks a rocky spit at Carry Point.

Ardlamont Point red can light buoy (*No. 47*) marks the east side of drying rocks and shoals extending up to 4 cables south of Ardlamont Point. The extremity of these shoals is WSW of the buoy, so that if coming from or going to Loch Fyne keep at least ¼ mile south of the point.

The West Kyle is often subject to squalls particularly, in westerly winds, off Kames where the wind funnels through a valley west of the village.

Light buoys

The buoys at the fish cages north of Rubha Ban are lit Fl.Y.6s at the north end and Fl.Y.4s at the south end.

Rubha Ban (*No. 45*) Fl.R.4s
Carry Rock (*No. 46*) Fl.R.4s
Ardlamont Point (*No. 47*) Fl.R.4s

There is no light at Rubha Dubh, but from southward it should show up against the lights at the villages.

Anchorages

Tighnabruaich, 55°54'·5N 5°13'·5W, has less suitable depth for anchoring except off the boatyard ¼ mile west of Rubha Ban. HIDB moorings are laid in several places off the village. Shops, post office, phone, hotel. Kyles of Bute Boatyard, ☎ Tighnabruaich (0700) 811213.

Black Farland Bay, on Bute, opposite Tighnabruaich provides good anchorage about the middle of the bay. A rock spit extends ½ cable offshore 3 cables northeast of Rubha Dubh, and a drying and shoal spit extends a cable off Rubha Glas, 7 cables northeast of Rubha Dubh.

Kames, 55°53'·5N 5°14'W, has HIDB visitors' moorings off the pier. Alternatively anchor clear of moorings, between Kames and Tighnabruaich piers, but as elsewhere the bottom drops away steeply. Shop, post office, phone, hotel.

Blindman's Bay is a mile north of Ardlamont Point buoy. Anchor in not less than 5 metres to avoid swinging into shoal water inshore.

Ettrick Bay on Bute, has underwater obstructions charted and reported to extend close inshore.

Inchmarnock and the west side of Bute

Except at Inchmarnock itself all anchorages are exposed to the southwest and are only suitable for occasional use.

Dangers and marks

Shearwater rock, depth 0·9 metres, is ½ mile southeast of Inchmarnock and rather west of midchannel; otherwise the coast of Bute is free of hazards outwith ¼ mile from the shore. A clearing line for the east side of Shearwater rock is to keep Northpark, a farmhouse near the north end of Inchmarnock, open of the east point of Inchmarnock, but the east point is difficult to identify.

Anchorages

Inchmarnock anchorage is off Midpark farm at the east side of the island.

St Ninian's Bay, east of Inchmarnock is clean but rocks dry for a cable inside its west point, and the head of the bay dries 3 cables.

Scalpsie Bay, 2 miles ESE of the south end of In-chmarnock, has cables occupying its eastern half, but a reasonable depth for anchoring can be found 2 cables off the farm on the northwest side. Shoals extend ¼ mile south from Ardscalpsie Point at the west of the entrance.

Lower Loch Fyne

Charts

2381 (1:25,000), *2131* (1:75,000) OS map *62*

Tides

Tidal streams are not significant in the lower loch.

Dangers and marks

The fairway of the loch as far as the approaches to Loch Gilp and Otter Spit is completely clean as are the shores outwith a cable. There are few marks of any sort; Tarbert is hidden but Barmore Island, 1½ miles NNW of Tarbert entrance is conspicuous. Detached drying rocks extend a cable east and 2 cables north of Barmore. Ardrishaig is also conspicuous.

Trials moorings joined by subsurface wires may be laid 1 mile off the west shore 2 miles north of Barmore, and 1 mile off the east shore at Kilfinan Bay 3½ miles NNE of Barmore. A mooring buoy is laid ½ mile SSE of Barmore.

Lamont Shelf 'safe water' buoy is 1½ miles SSE of Ardlamont Point. Skate Island (Sgat Mor) light beacon is off the east shore of the loch opposite south of Tarbert. Ardrishaig breakwater light beacon is very inconspicuous. Otter Spit light beacon in the entrance to Upper Loch Fyne is green, cylindrical.

Passage notes

The passage is straightforward, the only possible difficulty being the exposure by contrast with shelter in the Kyles or in the Crinan Canal. A steep sea can build up off Ardlamont Point, or in the mouth of Loch Gilp in a southerly wind.

Lights

Lamont Shelf buoy Fl(2)10s
Skate Island (Sgat Mor) light beacon Fl.3s9m12M
Mooring buoy SSE of Barmore Fl.Y.3s
Ardrishaig Breakwater LFl.WRG.6s9m4M
Otter Spit light beacon Fl.G.3s7m8M

East shore of Loch Fyne, looking north. Glenan Bay to the right.

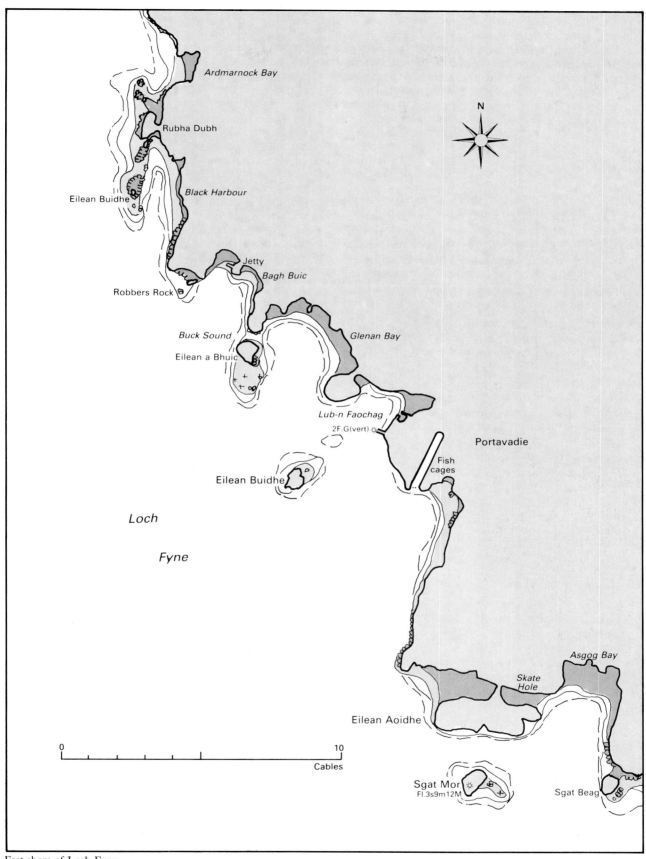

Ardmarnock Bay

Rubha Dubh

N

Eilean Buidhe

Black Harbour

Jetty

Bagh Buic

Robbers Rock

Buck Sound

Glenan Bay

Eilean a Bhuic

Lub-n Faochag

2F.G(vert)

Portavadie

Fish
cages

Eilean Buidhe

Loch

Fyne

Asgog Bay

Skate
Hole

Eilean Aoidhe

0   10
Cables

Sgat Mor
Fl.3s9m12M

Sgat Beag

East shore of Loch Fyne

Shelter

Tarbert provides good shelter from all directions but strong westerly winds tend to funnel through the gap from West Loch Tarbert and in these conditions it may be difficult to make the entrance. Ardrishaig gives shelter in the sea lock (unless, unusually, the gates are closed) except in strong east or northeast winds, when Tarbert would be easy to approach.

Tides

Constant +0005 Greenock (+0120 Dover)

Height in metres

MHWS	MHWN	MTL	MLWN	MLWS
3·4	2·9	1·9	1·1	0·3

Occasional anchorages on east shore of Loch Fyne

In light or offshore winds several bays on the east side of Loch Fyne provide attractive occasional anchorages and there are passages inshore of some of the islets. No supplies or services are available at any of these places.

Ardlamont Bay and Kilbride Bay, 1 and 2 miles respectively northwest of Ardlamont Point, have sandy beaches off which to anchor by day.

Sgat Mor, an island 10 metres high has a white light beacon on it; further north the islands and bays may be difficult to distinguish, but it is essential to do so to identify various drying and submerged rocks.

Asgog Bay, northeast of Sgat Mor (Skate Island) dries up to 1½ cables at the head and the bottom drops quickly from the LW line. Anchor in the northeast or northwest corner, or northeast of the east end of Eilean Aoidhe, in the mouth of an inlet known as Skate Hole.

The passage north of Sgat Mor is straightforward, but there is a submerged rock over a cable southeast of the northeast point of the island and a drying rock ½ cable southeast of the same point.

Portavadie, 1½ miles north of Sgat Mor, was developed as a yard for building oil rigs, but no orders materialised and it was abandoned. It is identified by steel sheet piling at the entrance to the artificial basin, and blocks of houses built for employees of the yard. The basin has deep water but the entrance is blocked by buoys and floating ropes.

There is some shelter behind the breakwater northwest of the basin. The wharf east of the breakwater is not convenient for small boats, and the harbour behind the wharf dries out. There are fish cages in Lub-n Faochag, the bay northwest of Portavadie.

Buck Bay from east.

Glenan Bay, the next bay northwest of Lub-n Faochag, has the familiar features of a foreshore drying up to a cable, and the bottom dropping sharply from the LW line, but it is possible to anchor off the east and northwest sides.

Eilean Buidhe, west of Portavadie, has drying and submerged rocks, particularly off its northeast side, and Eilean a Bhuic, south of the northwest point of Glenan Bay, has drying and submerged rocks up to 1½ cables south of it. Buck Rock, near the outer limit of these rocks, dries 3·4 metres and therefore rarely covers, but these rocks and the rocks off Eilean Buidhe need to be taken into account when approaching or leaving Portavadie or Glenan Bay.

Buck Sound, the passage between Eilean a Bhuic and the shore is clean.

Bagh Buic (Buck Bay), north of Eilean a Bhuic, is identified by a large modern house on its northeast side, and there are reasonable depths for anchoring in front of the house. Robber's Rock dries 1·8 metres 1 cable south of the northwest point of the bay; remember also the rocks around Eilean a Bhuic south of the bay.

Black Harbour, about ½ mile northwest of Buck Bay, has some shelter behind a low islet (also named Eilean Buidhe) and drying rocks but there are moderate depths at the head of the inlet.

Ardmarnock Bay is separated from Black Harbour by a small peninsula, Rubha Dubh. Rocks above water and drying extend north from the south point of the bay. The north point is clean and there is a boathouse with a slip there. The head of the bay dries, but there are moderate depths for anchoring at the south end.

Buck Sound from northwest.

Robber's Rock   Eilean a'Bhuie

Ardmarnock Bay from northeast.

Tarbert

55°52′N 5°24′W

One of the most completely sheltered harbours on the west coast of Scotland, but crowded with moorings, and with a bottom of soft mud. In westerly winds squalls are funnelled through the gap from West Loch Tarbert.

Tides

Constant +0005 Greenock (+0120 Dover)

Height in metres

MHWS	MHWN	MTL	MLWN	MLWS
3·4	2·9	1·9	1·1	0·3

Marks and approach

The main channel, south of Eilean a'Choich (Cock Island), is a third of a cable wide. A reef extending from the south shore ½ cable east of Cock Island, Madadh Maol, is marked by a red light column, and reefs off the south side of Cock Island by a green light column. A drying rock a third of a cable WSW of Cock Island is marked by a green perch with a triangular topmark.

Fishing boats use the main channel often at a considerable speed, and an alternative passage is north of Cock Island, but there is a large area of drying and above-water rocks, Sgeir Bhuidhe, northwest of the island. A green conical buoy marks shoal water off Leac Buidhe, the point of the mainland northeast of Cock Island; a red can buoy marks the northeast point of Sgeir Bhuidhe. A red perch is near the northwest point of Sgeir Bhuidhe.

Lights

Madadh Maol light column shows Fl.R.2·5s4m

The column south of Cock Island shows Q.G.3m
  These two lights in line lead to the entrance clear of the north shore.

The perch WSW of Cock Island is unlit (the first two lights in line astern lead clear south of this perch).

A stone dolphin towards the head of the harbour shows Fl.G.5s4m.

Mooring and anchorages

Pontoons are provided on the north side of the harbour and visitors should moor to the outside. Some moorings are provided by Tarbert Harbour Authority and the harbourmaster may be able to let you use one of these. There is unlikely to be space to anchor clear of moorings and clear of the approach to the pier. Mooring at the quay on the south side is permitted, but it is very much disturbed by fishing boats. In practice all except very large yachts should keep away.

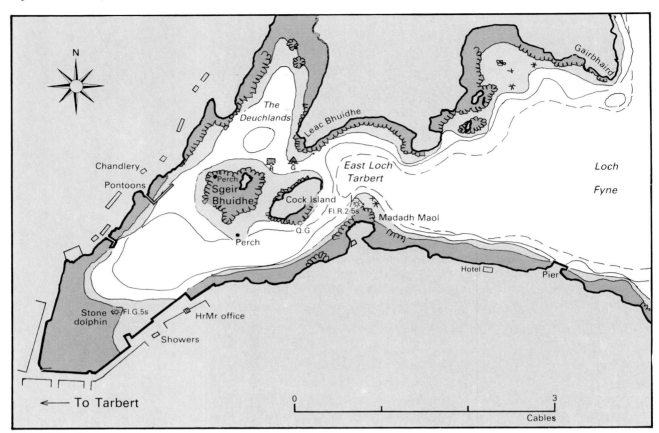

Tarbert

Tarbert Harbour entrance from southeast. Madadh Maol at bottom left, Leac Bhuidhe bottom right.

Tarbert Harbour from the west end; visitors' pontoons on the left.

Tarbert Harbour entrance. Madadh Maol on the left.

The Deuchlands (Dubh-chaol Linne), the northern arm of Tarbert harbour, may have space for anchoring, but there are drying rocks a cable from the head.

Outside the harbour, it is possible to anchor on the south side of the entrance, either off the Columba Hotel a cable west of the pier (the foreshore dries out ¼ cable and the bottom drops away sharply), or a cable east of the pier, off a house with a cupola where there is a wider area with reasonable depth but the bottom is uneven and rocky in places.

Supplies

Shops (EC Wednesday), post office, phone, hotels, *Calor Gas*, petrol, diesel, water at pier and at pontoons.

Services

Boatbuilder: A. MacCallum, ☎ Tarbert (08802) 209. Sailmaker, chandler and chart agent: W. B. Leitch, near pontoons, ☎ Tarbert (08802) 287. Showers, coin-operated, at toilet block at southwest end of main quay. Laundrette at Leitch's.

Communications

Harbourmaster's office is near the east end of the main quay, ☎ Tarbert (08802) 344, VHF Ch 16.

Barmore Island

The peninsula 1¼ miles north of the entrance to East Loch Tarbert has rocks above water and drying up to a cable east and 1½ cables northeast of it. A black over yellow beacon with a triangular topmark has been established by the Clyde Cruising Club on Sgeir Mhada Cinn, northeast of Barmore, but rocks extend a short way beyond the beacon. There are occasional anchorages southwest and northwest of Barmore.

South Bay is clean but its head dries for two cables. Anchor west of a small islet southwest of Barmore.

In North Bay, keep half a cable off the beacon and anchor, if suitable depth can be found, clear of the hotel's moorings, or if visiting the hotel, pick up one of the moorings.

Loch Gilp

An open, gradually shoaling, loch which dries for nearly a mile at the head, and in which a steep sea builds in southerly winds. Submerged rocks in the entrance are marked by two buoys.

Big Rock, 7 cables off the west shore 2¾ miles south of Ardrishaig breakwater has a depth of 2·1 metres.

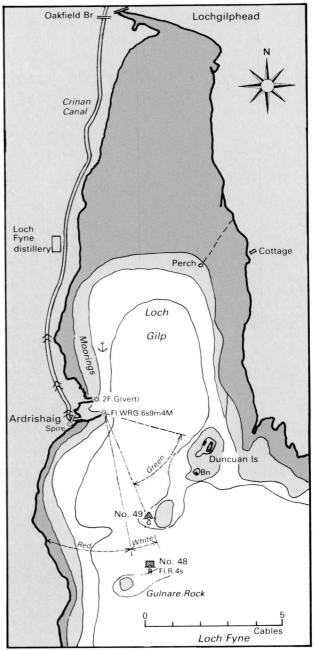

Loch Gilp

Tides

Constant (Tarbert) +0005 Greenock (+0120 Dover)

Height in metres

MHWS	MHWN	MTL	MLWN	MLWS
3·4	2·9	1·9	1·1	0·3

Dangers and marks

The buoys should be identified and the red can buoy *No. 48* left to port, and the green conical *No. 49* 1¾ cables north of it, left to starboard. Inspection of the chart will show that at suitable rise of tide and sea conditions alternative courses may be taken. Keep a reasonable distance off the end of the

Red light buoy   Breakwater head   Green conical buoy

Loch Gilp approach.

breakwater as it has rock footings; also a boat might be coming out from behind it.

Duncuan Island has a passage nearly a cable wide between it and the east shore but there are drying rocks off the east shore and shoal patches up to ½ cable north and southeast of the island. A rock drying 3 metres, ¾ cable SSW of Duncuan, is marked by a green beacon and there is a clear passage over a cable wide between the beacon and submerged rocks further southwest.

Lights

Ardrishaig breakwater light LFl.WRG.6s9m4M at its outer end; white over the fairway, red to the west and green to the east. It is difficult to identify against town lights.

No. 48 red can buoy, Fl.R.4s, is in the middle of the white sector, as is part of Gulnare Rock, 2·4 metres.

No. 49 buoy, which is not lit, is on the edge of the green sector.

Ardrishaig Pier has 2F.G(vert) lights

Entrance to canal sea lock is marked by F.R and F.G lights

Ardrishaig

There is no good anchorage or mooring in Ardrishaig Harbour, but the canal sea lock is normally left open (see below); a temporary berth can be found at the pier but fender boards will be needed. The north side of the breakwater dries along most of its length.

The regular anchorage is off the west shore north of the pier. The low water line is ½ mile north of the pier, on a line running west from a black and yellow sewer outfall beacon 1½ cables off a cottage on the east shore.

Communications

Canal office ☎ Lochgilphead (0546) 3210. VHF Ch 74.

Supplies

Shops, post office, phone, hotels, bank, *Calor Gas*, petrol diesel (at garage), paraffin at newspaper shop. Water taps around canal basin (with hoses) and at pier. Showers at pier (coin-operated, ask for key from lock-keeper). Chandlery and boatbuilder, ☎ Lochgilphead (0546) 3280.

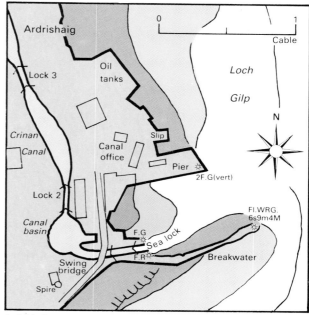

Ardrishaig

More shops, etc. at Lochgilphead (EC Tuesday at Lochgilphead, Wednesday at Ardrishaig). If passing through the canal, Lochgilphead is only a third of a mile from Oakfield Bridge.

Occasional anchorages

Glac Mhor and Glac Bheag, at the south end of the peninsula between Loch Gilp and Upper Loch Fyne, either side of Eilean Mor. Glac Mhor, east of Eilean Mor, is protected from the east by Liath Eilean. The very narrow passage, Dorus More, between an islet north of Liath Eilean and the mainland is shoal on either side.

Ardrishaig breakwater

73

Ardrishaig Harbour from east.

Ardrishaig Harbour from west. The sea lock is at the right.

Crinan Canal

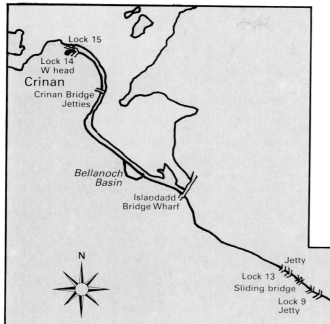

A local man may be hired, and his experience will be found valuable; ask at the canal office (or if going the other way, the duty lock-keeper at Crinan). To avoid delay it is worth arranging help in advance, through the canal office.

Ardrishaig Canal Basin is very small and vessels have to make a right-angle turn between the sea lock and lock *No. 2*; yachts moored there may be subject to minor damage. To leave a boat for several nights or longer consult the lock-keeper; it may be preferable to lie above lock 2.

The sea lock is normally left open, day and night, and you can usually go straight in unless it is filling or emptying or you are directed to stand off. Make ready warps and fenders before approaching. There are ladders on both sides. There is often quite a

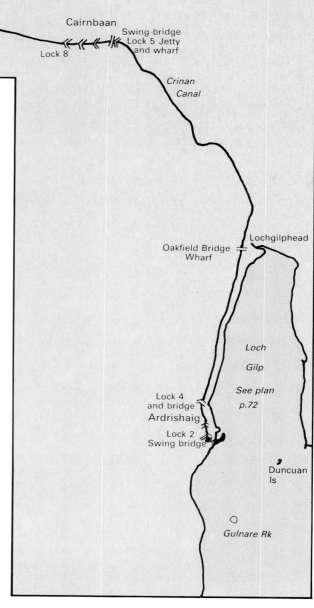

The canal through the neck of the Kintyre peninsula avoids the exposed passage round the Mull of Kintyre and, if coming from the upper part of the Firth, saves a distance of about 80 miles.

All locks apart from sea locks are worked by the boat's crew. The operation of gates and sluices takes considerable strength.

The passage through the canal is not without its hazards, and care is needed in positioning and handling fenders and warps, and managing a boat often in company with others which may be less than expertly handled, and possibly with a head or cross wind. Both luck and good management are needed to pass through the canal in less than six hours.

The scenery along the canal is extremely attractive and the passage can make a pleasant change from normal seafaring; it is worth taking it at a leisurely pace.

British Waterways Board provide a leaflet instructing yachts' crews in the operation of the canal, and this should be followed. It is essential to have an adequate number of stout fenders; four are barely adequate and you may regret not having eight. Two strong warps are needed, each about 20 metres in length, with a large soft eye or a bowline at the landward end.

Under good conditions two experienced people can take an easily managed boat through the canal, but it is preferable to have four. Don't rely on crews of other boats to help out, they may be short-handed too. I once helped an elderly couple take a boat through the canal; three other boats came through with us, each with two people on board, and none of them helped with the shore work.

strong current out of the lock from the runoff from the canal, so it is best to get the bow warp ashore first; however if the lock-keeper is standing by to take your warps he may insist on taking the stern warp, in which case keep some way on to stem the current and avoid being swung across the lock. There may be no-one to take ropes at all, so have a crew member ready to go up the ladder. Ropes should be led well fore and aft to keep the boat under control.

If there is a shortage of water (which, although it may seem surprising, is not uncommon) the use of the sea lock may be limited to half tide and above. Too much water running off the land into the canal may make the gates impossible to open.

Crinan Canal at lock 9 looking northwest.

Bellanoch Basin, looking southeast.

The sea lock is operated by a lock-keeper. While the lock is filling keep both warps tight; the bow warp may have to be led to a winch or windlass to control the boat.

At all 'inland' locks it is usual to take the stern warp ashore first to check way on entering the lock, but during and after heavy rain there may be a strong current out of the lock. Let the water in gradually to begin with and beware of helpful by-standers (I once saw a boat's bowsprit caught under the framing of a lock gate when a retired 'puffer' skipper opened both sluices together and the boat was driven forward uncontrollably by the backwash; there were some tense moments while the sluices were closed and the boat's transom hung over the bow of the boat astern).

There are seven swing (or sliding) bridges operated by keepers, four of these are at locks.

The lock before Crinan Basin, *No. 14*, has very rough sides and needs extra care with fenders.

Hours of operation

Seven days a week between May and September: sea locks 0600–2130, inland locks and bridges 0800–1615, both with a lunch break from 1200–1230. Locking may be arranged outside these hours at extra cost, but there are proposals to extend the operating time.

Services

Small shop/post office at Cairnbaan and at Bellanoch Bridge. Garage at Bellanoch Bridge. Boatyard, chandlery, hotel and coffee shop, diesel, petrol, water and *Calor Gas* at Crinan. No food shop, but a few provisions stocked at the chandlery.

Mooring

Transit jetties are provided at most locks, and boats may be moored for longer periods at Ardrishaig, Oakfield Bridge, Cairnbaan, Bellanoch Basin and Crinan, by arrangement with canal staff.

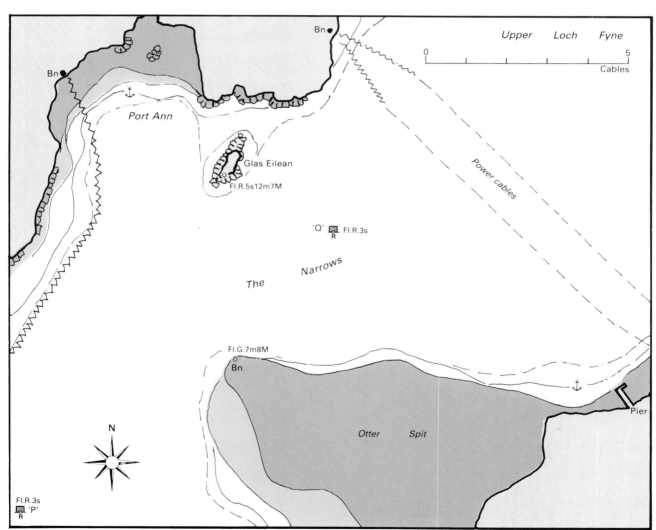

Upper Loch Fyne

Upper Loch Fyne

Chart

2382 (1:25,000)

Upper Loch Fyne is entered about 3 miles east of Ardrishaig by the west side of Otter Spit which dries for more than half the width of The Narrows from the east shore. The loch winds among hills for over 20 miles northeast from Otter Spit and is generally clean, apart from the spit itself and rocks at Minard Narrows, 6½ miles northeast of the spit.

Tides

Streams at The Narrows run at 1 knot at springs, turning at HW and LW Greenock, but close to the end of Otter Spit streams, especially on the ebb, run at up to 2 knots.

Constant (Inveraray) +0011 Greenock (+0126 Dover)

Height in metres

MHWS	MHWN	MTL	MLWN	MLWS
3·3	3·0	1·7	0·5	0·2

Dangers and marks

Otter Spit is marked at its west end by a green cylindrical light beacon 11 metres high. A submerged rock 7 cables southwest of the light beacon is marked on its northeast side by a red can light buoy, marked '*P*'. Glas Eilean, ½ mile north of Otter Spit beacon, has a red light column at its south end. The red light buoy '*Q*' is of no significance to yachts. Clach Garbh, 1½ miles north of Otter Spit beacon, is a rock drying 1·5 metres, a cable off the west shore.

Passage

Pass east of buoy '*P*' and at least ½ cable west of Otter Spit beacon. If going against the tide keep further off the beacon as the tide runs more strongly there.

Lights

Otter Spit beacon shows Fl.G.3s7m8M
Glas Eilean shows Fl.R.5s12m7M
Both buoys '*P*' and '*Q*' are lit Fl.R.3s

Shelter

Loch Gair is well sheltered with easy access by day.

Occasional anchorages

Port Ann is an anchorage for light or offshore winds; the head dries off for over a cable. Underwater cables occupy part of the west shore of the bay, southward of a cable beacon.

Otter Spit from northeast. The light beacon is towards the top right-hand corner and the old ferry pier is at the bottom left.

Otter Ferry, northwest of a stone pier which is a mile east of Otter Spit beacon. Less than 2 cables northeast of the pier several underwater power cables cross the loch, marked by a beacon on the shore.

Shops, post office, telephone, hotel, *Calor Gas* at Largiemore caravan site, 1 mile north. Petrol. Water at craft shop.

Loch Gair

An enclosed pool on the west shore 3 miles north of Otter Spit beacon, easy to enter in daylight and identified by the Pointhouse, a rectangular white tower on the south side of the entrance.

A spit at the inner end of the entrance channel on the north side dries out 1 cable; keep closer to the south side until past the point 2 cables northwest of the Pointhouse. The foreshore is muddy and the loch is shoal on all sides; at LW the point 2 cables northwest of the Pointhouse is the cleanest place at which to land.

Supplies

Shop, post office, telephone, hotel. Showers at hotel. Hotel has two moorings.

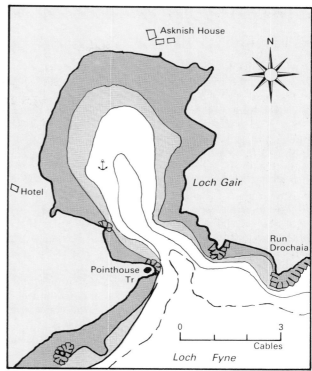

Loch Gair

Loch Gair from east. The inner spit on the northeast side can be a bad trap towards high water.

Minard Narrows

6½ miles ENE of Otter Spit several islets, rocks and banks, both drying and submerged, are spread across the loch. Eilean Aoghainn and Fraoch Eilean constitute the main group with rocks drying and submerged up to 2 cables NNE, marked by 'X' red can light buoy on their east side.

Sgeir an Eirionnaich, 2 cables ENE of the light buoy, has a cylindrical metal light beacon 7 metres high. Otter Rock (An Oitir), 1 metre high, 1½ cables west of Eilean Aoghainn has a gravel bank drying 1½ cables WNW of it, marked at its WNW end by a black beacon with a spherical topmark.

The main passage is between Sgeir an Eireonnaich and the red light buoy, but others may be taken with careful attention to the chart.

Lights

Sgeir an Eirionnaich Fl.WR.3s7m8M, showing red over the rocks north of Eilean Aoghainn, and also over a shoal to the NNE which is of no concern to yachts. The red light buoy 'X' shows Fl.R.3s.

Anchorages

Minard Bay is the best anchorage in this part of the loch, ½ mile west of Fraoch Eilean. Other occasional anchorages on the west side are at Auch-goyle Bay, 8 cables NNW of Eilean Aoghainn, south of Minard village, and Crarae Bay, 1½ miles north of Eilean Aoghainn and ½ mile south-west of a disused quarry. Some supplies at Minard.

Furnace, on the northwest shore, 3½ miles northeast of Eilean Aoghainn, has a very conspicuous active quarry. At night, the quarry jetty shows 2F.R(vert) lights.

Other occasional anchorages

Throughout the upper loch occasional anchorages can be found on the chart, but many bays are too deep or shoal. Those most useful are as follows, all on the southeast shore:

Newton, opposite Furnace, either behind the island Innavagaan to the west of Newton village, or off the east end of the village. The shore in front of the main part of the village dries 1 cable.

Strachur, 3 miles ENE of Furnace, off the south end of the bay; the northeast side of the bay dries over a cable. Admiralty mooring buoy. Shop, post office, telephone, hotel. In an area between 1 and 2½ miles NNE of Strachur anchoring is prohibited.

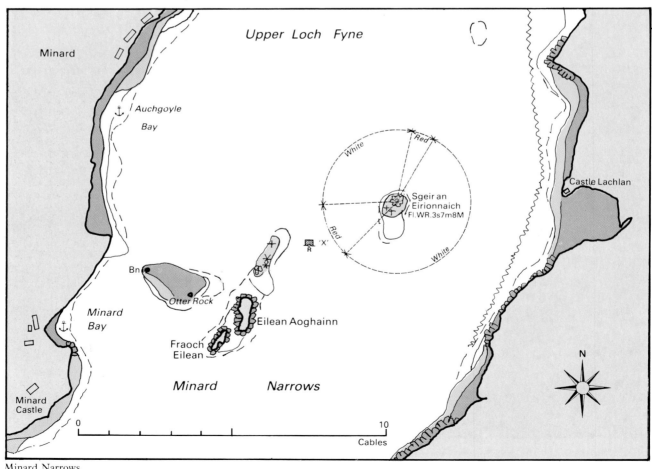

Minard Narrows

St Catherine's, opposite Inveraray, ¼ mile southwest of the hotel.

Cairndow has an extensive raft of fish cages lying in the middle of the loch off Ardkinglas House, marked by cardinal buoys at its south and north points. Anchor ¾ mile from the head of the loch, off the north end of the village; the shore in front of the village dries for a cable.

Inveraray

An 18th-century planned town, one of the west coast's principal tourist attractions. Inveraray Castle, a 19th-century mansion, is open to the public. A drying harbour is formed by the pier at the northeast point of the village.

Tides

Constant (Inveraray) +0011 Greenock (+0126 Dover)

Height in metres

MHWS	MHWN	MTL	MLWN	MLWS
3·3	3·0	1·7	0·5	0·2

Dangers and marks

A drying spit, An Oitir, extends 2 cables from the northwest shore southwest of Inveraray. The two-arched bridge north of Inveraray open of the pier 355° leads clear of the spit.

Anchorage

The shore north of Inveraray dries nearly as far as the pierhead but there are suitable depths for anchoring in Newtown Bay, between An Oitir and Inveraray. The position of the inner end of An Oitir is indicated by an 'Esso' garage sign at the south end of a row of houses at Newton.

Supplies

Shops, post office, telephone, hotel, *Calor Gas*, petrol and diesel at garage south of village. Water at toilet block at the pier.

Inveraray from south. The two-arched bridge on the right in line with the head of the pier clears An Oitir.

V. Kintyre and Kilbrannan Sound

Charts

2126, 2131, 2168 (1:75,000), *2221* (1:36,000), OS maps *62, 68*

The peninsula of Kintyre extends 40 miles or so south from the mainland, protecting the Firth of Clyde from the open Atlantic, and leaving a gap of 11 miles between its extremity, the Mull of Kintyre, and the Irish coast. The difference between the times of high water west of Kintyre and in the Firth of Clyde cause strong tidal streams off the Mull; the swell and the prevailing westerly winds ensure that conditions inshore are rarely peaceful. The simple tactic of passing the point well offshore conflicts with the requirement to keep clear of a Traffic Separation Scheme the east end of which is only 2 miles southwest of the Mull of Kintyre.

Between the Clyde and the west coast of Scotland the passage round the Mull presents a challenge, but now that the Crinan Canal operates regularly on Sundays there is always an alternative. However, many local yachtsmen still prefer to go round the Mull; some consider the canal to be more of a challenge!

Between the North Channel and the west coast of Scotland the obvious passage is outside the Mull, but if the weather is unfavourable you can take the alternative route by way of Kilbrannan Sound and the Crinan Canal.

The sequence followed in this chapter is through Kilbrannan Sound from north to south; Campbeltown Loch; round the Mull of Kintyre and northwards along the west side of Kintyre to Gigha and West Loch Tarbert.

Shelter

Campbeltown Loch provides excellent shelter (although some sea works in with strong easterly winds) and easy access by day or night. Carradale Harbour in Kilbrannan Sound provides shelter except from strong northerly winds. Gigha provides shelter except from the east; see also Chapter VI for Islay.

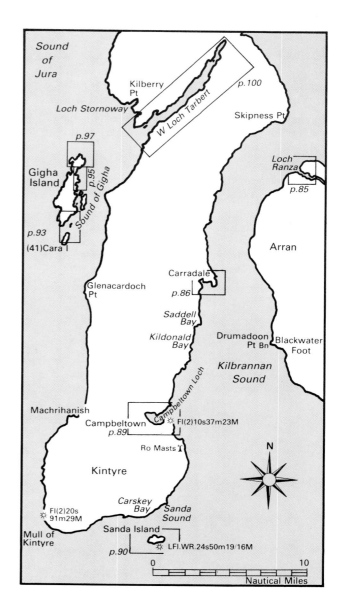

Kilbrannan Sound

55°35′N 5°25′W

In the passage between the east side of Kintyre and the island of Arran any wind tends to be deflected along the line of the sound and increased in velocity. Erins Bank in the middle of the north part of the sound causes overfalls. Tidal streams generally do not exceed ½ knot.

Chart

2126, 2131 (1:75,000), *2221* (1:36,000), OS map *69*

Dangers and marks

Skipness Point at the north end of the sound has a red can light buoy off its south side, and radio masts and light beacons 1½ miles north of the point.

Carradale Point on the west side of the sound is prominent and has a red can light buoy off its southeast point.

Ross Island, a rock with a jagged outline nearly 4 miles north of Island Davaar is conspicuous from north or south.

Iron Rock Ledges, submerged and drying rocks, extend several cables off the southwest side of Arran from Pladda to Blackwaterfoot and are marked by a green conical light buoy nearly a mile offshore, 7 miles west of Pladda.

Otterard Rock with a least depth of 3·2 metres, northeast of the entrance to Campbeltown Loch is marked by an east cardinal light buoy. Rocks inshore 1¼ miles north of Island Davaar are marked by a red can buoy.

Island Davaar lighthouse is a conspicuous white tower 20 metres high on Island Davaar at the south side of the entrance to Campbeltown Loch.

Lights

Skipness Calibration Range, ¾ mile NNE of Skipness Point shows Iso.R.8s7m10M 292°-vis-312°, together with an Oc(2)Y.10s24M when the range is in use.
Skipness Point light buoy Fl.R
Carradale Point light buoy Fl(2)R.12s
Iron Rock Ledges light buoy Fl.G.6s
Otterard Rock east cardinal light buoy Q(3)10s
Island Davaar lighthouse Fl(2)10s37m23M

Loch Ranza

55°43′N 5°18′W

A popular anchorage at the northwest of Arran but subject to violent squalls in offshore winds. Drying and submerged rocks extend about a cable south of Newton Point at the north side of the entrance.

Loch Ranza from north-northwest.

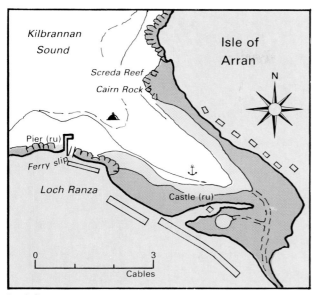

Loch Ranza

The pier at the south side of the entrance is ruined and unsafe, and a car ferry operates from a slip at the east side of the pier. At night the ferry usually lies at a mooring in the middle of the loch, but sometimes inside the head of the pier.

The bottom, particularly on the north side is very soft mud, and dragging the anchor is a common experience there. The south shore dries out in places about a cable.

The pool east of the castle has a drying bar and a yacht on a mooring occupies the pool. Yachts able to dry out might have a quiet night aground there if the tide serves, but it should be inspected at low tide first.

Tides

Constant +0005 Greenock (+0120 Dover)

Height in metres

MHWS	MHWN	MTL	MLWN	MLWS
3·4	2·9	1·9	1·1	0·3

Supplies

Shops (licensed grocer, butcher), post office, telephone, hotel, *Calor Gas*, water at head of the ferry slip.

Moorings

Grogport 55°38'·5N 5°29'W: Visitors' moorings have been laid for the use of customers of a restaurant at this bay 3 miles north of Carradale. Water is available at the restaurant.

Head of Loch Ranza from southwest. Note how far the shoals extend from the shore.

Carradale harbour (Port Crannaich) from east.

Carradale Harbour (Port Crannaich)

55°36′N 5°28′W

A small harbour formed by a sheet-piled breakwater a mile north of Carradale Point. Nearly half the width of the harbour dries but there is about 3 metres alongside the breakwater. Fishing boats congregate here at weekends.

Light

Fl.R.10s5m6M at the end of the breakwater

Supplies

Shops, post office, telephone, hotels, *Calor Gas*, water, harbourmaster ☎ (058 33) 209. Fishermen's chandlery.

Torrisdale Bay and Carradale Bay

55°34′N 5°29′W

Depending on wind direction anchor as depth allows off Torrisdale Castle, a large stone house in the southwest corner of the bay, or in the northeast corner of Carradale Bay.

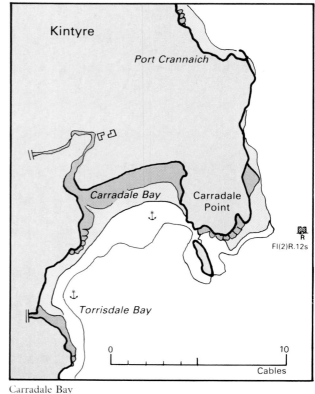

Carradale Bay

Torrisdale Bay from southeast.

Occasional anchorages in southern part of sound

Blackwaterfoot, on Arran ESE of Drumadoon Point, has a tiny boat harbour at the mouth of a river, where sailing coasters used to be towed in by rowing boats. The harbour might be used by trailer-sailers. There are shoal rocky patches offshore, but keel boats can anchor off the river mouth in quiet weather.

Saddell Bay, 2¾ miles south of Carradale Point.

Kildonald Bay, 2 miles south of Saddell Bay, with some shelter from south behind Ross Island, but there are drying rocks on the south side of the bay.

Campbeltown Loch

55°25'N 5°35'W

Chart

1864 (1:12,500), OS map *68*

Tides

Constant +0010 Greenock (+0125 Dover)

Height in metres

MHWS	MHWN	MTL	MLWN	MLWS
2·9	2·6	1·8	1·1	0·6

Directions

A well sheltered loch on the east side of Kintyre 9 miles north of Sanda Island, identified by a conspicuous lighthouse on the north side of Island Davaar at its entrance. 1½ miles NNE of Island Davaar lighthouse an east cardinal light buoy marks

87

Campbeltown Loch from Island Davaar. Millmore Beacon is at the extreme left. Trench Point is right of centre with Campbeltown Harbour beyond. The entrance is at the bottom right with Millbeg buoy at the extreme right and Millmore buoy about the centre of the photo.

Otterard Rock with a least depth of 3·2 metres. Rocks further inshore are marked by an unlit red can buoy.

The radio mast charted north of Trench Point is a lattice communications tower with dish aerials, but a tapering lattice mast ½ mile east of it is more conspicuous to a yacht approaching from the north.

Off the east side of Island Davaar tidal streams run at up to 2 knots on the flood (northward) and 3 knots on the ebb (southward) with overfalls off the southeast point of the island on the ebb. In strong onshore winds the sea surges round the north end of the island, so give it a good berth, as far as the middle of the channel.

Occasional anchorage in Kildalloig Bay southwest of Island Davaar with some shelter from northwest from the Dhorlin except at high water. An underwater cable, probably well buried, crosses the bay in about 3 metres.

A cable northeast of Macringan's Point on the north side of the entrance Yellow Rocks just dry, but are clear of the channel unless you are tacking or approaching from north very close inshore.

Millmore Bank, marked by a stone beacon and a red light buoy 4 cables west of Island Davaar, intrudes into the south side of the channel; a cable NNW of the red buoy a green light buoy marks the edge of Millbeg Bank on the north side of the channel.

West of Millmore Bank the loch opens out; *Methe Bank* RW light buoy 3 cables WSW of Millmore Beacon is of no significance to yachts. The NATO pier is prominent on the south shore.

The shipyard at Trench Point is prominent on the north shore and there is a green conical light buoy off the end of the point. A green conical beacon stands near the east end of a drying bank east of Trench Point.

Lights

Otterard Rock light buoy Q(3)10s
Island Davaar lighthouse Fl(2)10s37m23M, obscured from south of 330°
Millmore Bank light buoy Fl.R.10s
Millbeg Bank light buoy Fl.G.2·5s
Methe Bank light buoy Iso.10s
Trench Point light buoy Fl.G.6s
NATO Pier Q.R.7m2M at each end of head
Leading lights 240·3° on the south shore are both F.Y.7/28m6M
The naval mooring buoy ½ mile southeast of New Quay is unlit.
Lights at the harbour:
  New Quay 2F.R(vert)5m4M
  Old Quay 2F.G(vert)7m4M

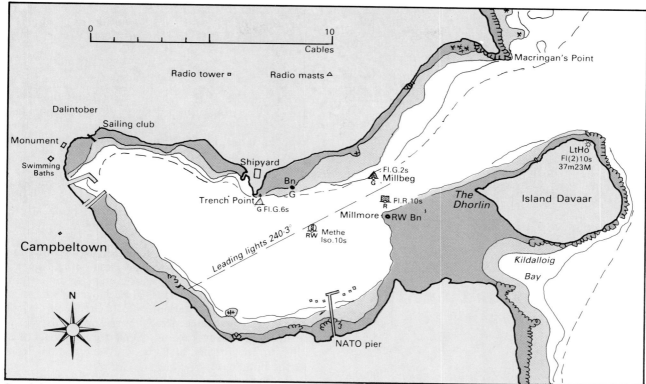

Campbeltown

Campbeltown Harbour

The harbour, on the southwest shore, consists of two stone quays 7 cables west of Trench Point, Old Quay to the northwest and New Quay to the southeast; the head of Old Quay is extensively used by coasters at present. Most of the harbour dries although part of its seaward side was dredged to 4m in 1983.

A very large mooring buoy lies 2 cables off the southwest shore ½ mile southeast of New Quay.

Berths

A finger pontoon is planned to be installed in the summer of 1989, as shown on the plan, but until the installation is complete the best berth is on the north side of Old Quay. If there are more than three boats abreast the way out for the lifeboat may be obstructed. These quays are heavily used by fishing boats and yachts may be asked to move.

Beyond the harbour the head of the loch is shoal; Campbeltown Sailing Club has moorings east of Dalintober Pier but no visitors' moorings.

Anchorages

Anchorage may be found between Old Quay and the sewer outfall towards Dalintober Pier, but taking care not to be too far inshore, and clear of access to Old Quay and the way out for the lifeboat. Alternatively about a cable offshore southeast of New Quay. About 4 cables west of NATO Pier the wreck of a submarine is a hazard. Yachts at anchor must show an anchor light as fishing boats use the harbour at night.

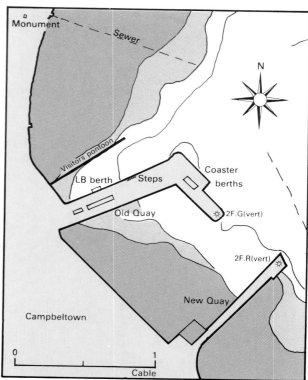

Campbeltown Harbour

Supplies and services

Shops, post office, bank, telephone, hotel, *Calor Gas*, petrol, diesel, water at southeast end of green shed on the head of Old Quay, EC Wednesday, harbourmaster ☎ Campbeltown (0586) 52552. Showers at swimming pool northwest of harbour (not open mornings at present), or at some hotels, and at Sailing Club.

Electronics and marine engineers at the harbour. Marine surveyor. Slip at harbour suitable for large motor yachts; small boats can dry out beside harbour wall.

Campbeltown Shipyard, ☎ Campbeltown (0586) 52881, can carry out hull, electrical and mechanical repairs.

Air service to Glasgow twice daily on weekdays; daily bus to Glasgow.

Sanda Sound and the Mull of Kintyre

Charts

2724 North Channel to the Firth of Lorne (1:200,000) is convenient for passage planning, but at a larger scale (1:75,000) three charts *2126*, *2199* and *2798* all overlap at the Mull.

Imray's chart *C63* takes you round the Mull to Gigha, and *C64* overlaps it, covering from Sanda Island to Islay and Colonsay, together with part of the Ulster coast.

Tides

In the middle of the North Channel and the Western Approaches spring tides run at over 3 knots and close inshore, over 5 knots. The inshore tides turn over an hour earlier than those offshore forming heavy overfalls in unsettled conditions at the boundary between the two streams.

At a point 2 miles SSW of the west end of Sanda the west-going stream begins about −0120 Greenock (HW Dover), and the east-going stream begins about +0440 Greenock (+0600 Dover). The spring rate in both directions is over 3 knots.

On the west side of Kintyre the north-going stream begins rather earlier and ends rather later.

In Sanda Sound the west-going stream begins about −0230 Greenock (−0110 Dover). The east-going stream begins about +0340 Greenock (+0500 Dover). In both directions this stream forms part of an inshore stream turning over an hour earlier than the streams further offshore with severe turbulence at the boundaries.

Races form on the ebb north of Sheep Island and north of Sanda.

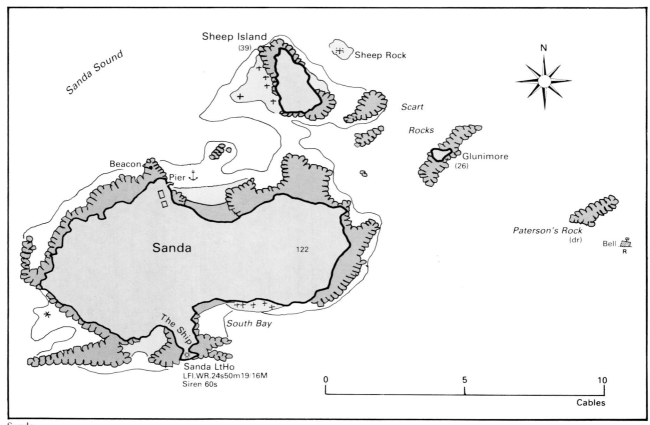

Sanda

Dangers and marks

Ru Stafnish on the east side of Kintyre, 5½ miles NNE of Sanda, is identified by three radio masts on a hill ½ mile to the west.

Apart from the general sea conditions the principal dangers are all near Sanda and Sanda Sound.

In Sanda Sound rocks awash and drying extend up to ¼ mile from the mainland from the Arranman Barrels 2¼ miles NNE of Sanda, marked by a red can light buoy, to Macosh Rock northwest of Sanda, also marked by a red can light buoy.

Dun na h-Oighe, a prominent knob on the shore west of Arranman Barrels is a useful reference point when coming from the north. A radio mast stands near the shore north of Macosh Rock buoy.

Sheep Island, north of Sanda, has drying rocks on all sides, those to the north extending ½ cable. Paterson's Rock dries a mile east of Sanda, marked by an unlit red can bell buoy.

Sanda Island lighthouse stands on a rocky promontory (known as 'The Ship') on the south side of Sanda at a height of 50 metres.

Mull of Kintyre lighthouse stands on a steep hillside on the west side of the Mull of Kintyre at a height of 90 metres and is not visible from east of 350°.

The eastern extremity of the Traffic Separation Scheme is 2¼ miles southwest of Mull of Kintyre lighthouse, limiting the distance off the point at which yachts may round the point unless passing along the northwest-going lane of the scheme.

Passage planning

Sanda, the only anchorage near the Mull, provides less than complete shelter, but is considered an excellent anchorage in settled conditions or if the wind is southerly. The bottom is clean sand and Sanda is used regularly as a staging post for yachts on passage round the Mull.

Distances between anchorages are more significant than is usual on the west coast of Scotland. The shortest distance between anchorages (other than Sanda) on a passage round the Mull is 44 miles.

The distance from a point 1 mile southeast of Arranman Barrels to a point 2 miles southwest of Mull of Kintyre lighthouse, is about 11 miles.

From Cove Point southeast of Arranman Barrels to Campbeltown Harbour is 11 miles, and to Lamlash Harbour on the east side of Arran 24 miles.

The distance from the point 2 miles southwest of Mull of Kintyre lighthouse to each of the following anchorages is about 24 miles: Ardminish Bay, Gigha; Loch an t-Sailein, Islay; Port Ellen, Islay.

Allow for sudden, not forecast, changes of weather partly because they are more inclined to happen at a turning point such as the Mull, and partly because the distance from shelter is greater than usual.

From the Clyde to the west side of Kintyre, if the wind is southwesterly, there is little point in using Sanda Sound. The tidal stream will be either against you or against the wind; no distance would be saved if tacking, and motoring would be uncomfortable (to say the least).

Local yachtsmen, however, usually take the inshore passages at Sanda and the Mull, preferring to endure discomfort and save distance. There are people who have been round the Mull many times and profess to find nothing to it, and others with the most picturesque horror stories. It depends, no doubt, partly on luck, and partly on the temperament of the storyteller.

The southwest-going tide sets across Paterson's Rock and the buoy is moored south of the rock. For a clearing mark, the east point of Island Davaar open of Ru Stafnish astern leads 1¾ miles east of Paterson's Rock.

Pass at least ½ mile east of Paterson's Rock buoy and a mile south of Sanda, or 2 miles off if the wind is more than Force 3; plan to be south of Sanda about the time that the tide turns to the west.

Resist the temptation to bear away when the Mull of Kintyre lighthouse comes into sight, and pass two miles off it, to avoid a south-going eddy inshore.

If the wind is northwesterly Sanda Sound can be used, but if it is any more than light, conditions will probably be unattractive when the west side of the Mull is opened up. Standing further offshore will take you into the Traffic Separation Scheme.

Moderate winds between northeast and south present little problem; if making for Gigha or the Sound of Jura in wind directions except between south and west aim to be at the east end of Sanda Sound 2½ hours before HW Greenock.

If making for Islay aim to be clear of the Mull of Kintyre by 4½ hours after HW Greenock, but if late keep well clear of the east-going stream inshore; an adverse tide in the deep water clear of the Mull is much weaker than near the shore.

Passages beyond the Mull are generally straightforward but if there is a heavy swell it will be steeper near the shore.

For the south and east of Islay, the Sound of Islay, and the Sound of Jura see the respective following chapters.

The passage eastward presents fewer problems if only in that easterly winds do not blow from the open sea, but a following westerly wind can build up overwhelming seas.

Lights around the Mull

At night the waters around the Mull of Kintyre are well provided with powerful lights, but in an area ENE of Sanda Sound three out of the four nearest lights are obscured. For more than 5 miles northeast of Sanda, Sanda Island lighthouse, Island Davaar and Ailsa Craig lights are all obscured, leaving only Pladda visible, at least 13 miles away, and the two light buoys in Sanda Sound.

Mull of Kintyre Fl(2)20s91m29M

Sanda Island LFl.WR.24s50m19/16M; flash is 8 seconds long. Light is obscured from northeast of 245°, red 245°-267° and white elsewhere.

Arranman Barrels buoy Fl(2)R.12s
Macosh Rock buoy Fl.R.6s
Paterson's Rock bell buoy is not lit.

More distant lights

Altacarry Head Fl(4)20s74m26M; the northeast point of Rathlin Island, 12 miles west of Mull of Kintyre

Rue Point Fl(2)5s16m14M; the southeast point of Rathlin Island

Island Davaar Fl(2)10s37m23M obscured from south of 330°; Campbeltown Loch, 9 miles north of Sanda

Ailsa Craig Fl(6)30s18m17M 028°-obscd-145°; 16 miles east of Sanda

Sanda Island

55°17'N 5°35'W

Tides

Constant −0040 Greenock (+0035 Dover)

Height in metres (estimated)

MHWS	MHWN	MTL	MLWN	MLWS
2·4	2·0	1·4	0·6	0·4

Anchorage

Sanda Island's anchorage is in a bay on the north side of the island. A reef at the west side of the bay is marked by a green iron beacon with a ball topmark, well inshore of the edge of the reef. There are drying rocks in the middle of the bay and at the southeast side. Enter from due north at the west side to avoid drying rocks and anchor northeast of the stone pier. Some swell is likely under most conditions.

Sanda anchorage from the south shore. *Photo M. B. Balmforth*

Other anchorages

Carskey Bay provides temporary anchorage on the mainland shore northwest of Sanda Island and is said to be clear of tide. It is off low ground at the mouth of a valley ¾ mile west of the conspicuous white hotel at Southend village. Carskey Rocks dry 2 cables off the west side of the bay and a submerged reef lies off Keil Point at its east side. Some supplies at Southend village.

South Bay, Sanda, east of the lighthouse, provides shelter from northwest winds, but rocks dry up to ¼ mile east of its southwest point.

Machrihanish Bay, on the west side of the Mull of Kintyre at the south end of sand dunes 7½ miles north of Mull of Kintyre lighthouse, provides temporary anchorage to wait for more favourable conditions to round the Mull, but can be a trap if the wind comes onshore, or particularly if any swell comes into the bay. Skerrivore rocks extend 4 cables northwest from the southwest point of the bay and there are submerged rocks up to 2 cables off the south shore. Anchor off the mouth of a burn at the southeast side of the bay. If conditions do not seem suitable for a passage round the Mull, it would be best not to leave Gigha or Islay.

Sound of Gigha

55°41'N 5°44'W

Gigha is a pleasantly pastoral island with famous subtropical gardens particularly worth visiting in May and June. The main anchorages are on the east side of the island and are uncomfortable in winds from that direction.

Charts

2475 (1:25,000), *2168* (1:75,000), OS map *62*

Tides

The north-going stream begins +0430 Oban (−0100 Dover), and the south-going stream begins −0200 Oban (+0500 Dover).

Constant is approximately −0200 Oban (+0500 Dover) at springs, and −0500 Oban (+0300 Dover) at neaps.

Height in metres

MHWS	MHWN	MTL	MLWN	MLWS
1·5	1·3	1·0	0·8	0·6

Directions

The sound has the reputation of being difficult to navigate but in moderate weather and reasonable visibility will present little difficulty. The usual passages and anchorages are on the west side of the sound and shoals and rocks near the mainland side are not described.

To make the information more digestible the approaches from the south and from the north are described separately.

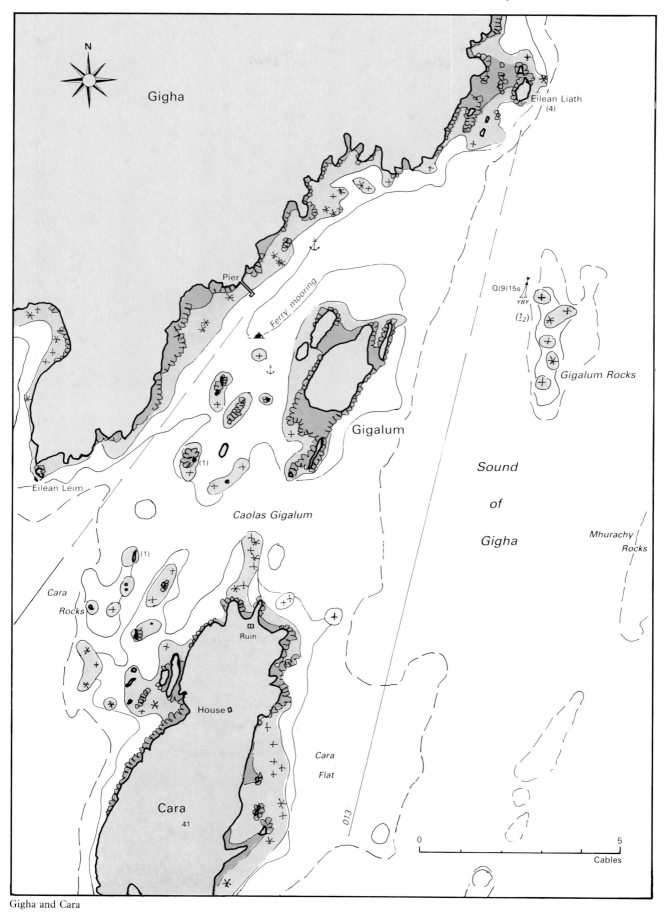

N

Gigha

Eilean Liath
(4)

Pier

Ferry mooring

Q(9)15s
YBY

(1₂)

Gigalum

Gigalum Rocks

Eilean Leim

Caolas Gigalum

Sound

of

Gigha

Mhurachy
Rocks

(1)

(1)

Cara
Rocks

Ruin

House

Cara
Flat

Cara
41

013

0   5

Cables

Gigha and Cara

Cara from south.

Dangers and marks at the south end of the sound

¾ mile off the mainland shore, southeast of Cara is an unmarked rock Sgeir an Tru, drying 1·2 metres.

The east side of Cara, the most southerly island off Gigha, is clean outwith ½ cable from its east shore, except for a submerged rock 1·8 metres just over a cable northeast of the island.

The east side of Gigalum, north of Cara is clean, and Gigalum Rocks, 4 cables east of Gigalum are marked on their west side by a west cardinal light buoy.

At Eilean Liath, a group of islets off the east side of Gigha ¾ mile NNE of Gigalum, there is a drying rock ½ cable ENE of Eilean Liath. Note the Wee Rocks east of Gigalum Rocks, and Sgeir Gigalum, about a mile northeast of the light buoy.

Approach from south

West side Keep at least a mile off the mainland shore to avoid Sgeir an Tru. Pass at least 2 cables east of Cara and steer to keep Eilean Liath ahead in line with Ardminish Point 1½ miles further north bearing 013°. Pass west of Gigalum Rocks buoy and alter course to pass a cable east of Eilean Liath.

East side The east side of the sound could be safely negotiated, once Sgeir an Tru is passed, by following the 10-metre contour.

Dangers and marks at the north end of the sound

An Dubh-sgeir, ½ mile north of Gigha is 3 metres high, with submerged and drying rocks around it.

Gamhna Gigha, 1¼ miles east of the north end of Gigha, is 2 metres high.

Badh Rock, 1½ miles south of Gamhna Gigha, is marked on its west side by an unlit west cardinal buoy.

Bhlar Rock (Sgeir Blath-shuileach), 8 cables WSW of Badh Rock, 1 metre high, is the north end of a reef extending nearly a mile from the east side of Druimyeon Bay.

Sgeir Nuadh which dries 1·2 metres, 3 cables southeast of Bhlar Rock, is probably the most dangerous rock in the sound as it is unmarked and right in the fairway.

Approach from north

Identify Gamhna Gigha and then Badh Rock buoy and pass within a cable west of it. Continue heading south for half a mile before altering course towards Eilean Liath to avoid Sgeir Nuadh.

A traditional leading line based on a ruin on Cara can be misleading because the ruin referred to is unidentifiable, and if Cara House were mistaken for it you would be led close to Sgeir Nuadh.

If, in clear weather, you pass near the northeast point of Gigha and can identify Bhlar Rock on the horizon ahead, you may prefer to pass west of Sgeir Nuadh or straight into the north end of Druimyeon Bay.

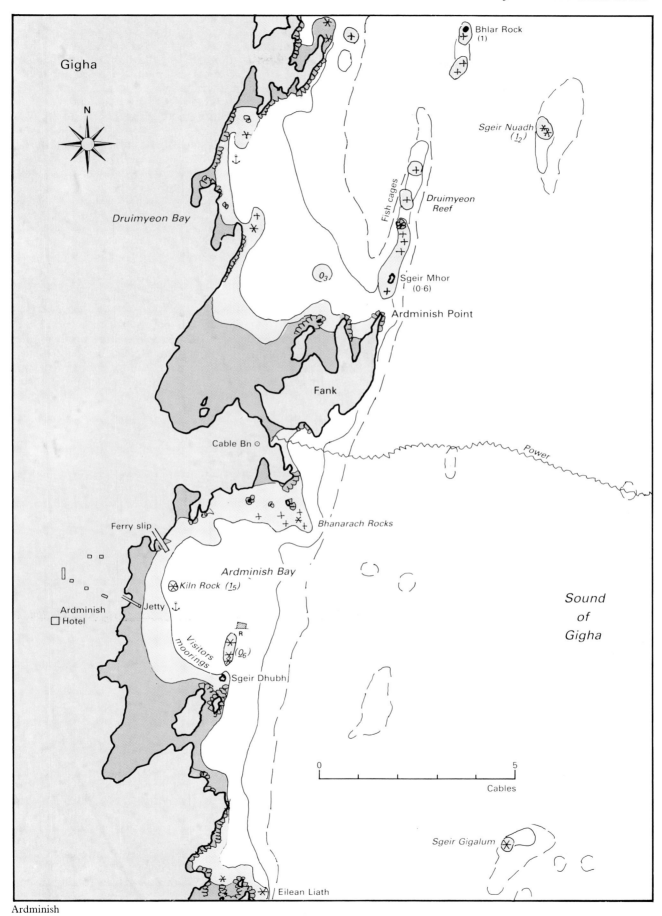

Gigha

N

Druimyeon Bay

Bhlar Rock
(1)

Sgeir Nuadh
(*1*₂)

Fish cages

Druimyeon
Reef

(0₃)

Sgeir Mhor
(0·6)

Ardminish Point

Fank

Cable Bn ⊙

Power

Ferry slip

Bhanarach Rocks

Ardminish Bay

Kiln Rock (*1*₅)

R
(*0*₆)

Ardminish
Hotel

Jetty

Visitors
moorings

Sgeir Dhubh

Sound
of
Gigha

0   5

Cables

Sgeir Gigalum

Eilean Liath

Ardminish

To leave Gigha Sound from Ardminish by the north steer to keep Badh Rock buoy on the port bow, bearing not more than 030°, until it is in line with Gamhna Gigha and then pass west of the buoy.

Lights

Gigalum Rocks west cardinal buoy is lit Q(9)15s.
A row of five street lights at Ardminish ferry slip are normally left on at night.

Caolas Gigalum

55°39′N 5°45′W

Caolas Gigalum, the sound separating Cara and Gigalum from Gigha, is full of rocks, most of them above water but less than a metre high. The simplest approach is from the north. Anchor no closer to Gigha than the end of the pier.

Rocks, mostly above water extend ¼ mile WNW of Cara, leaving a passage 3 cables wide southeast of Gigha, but the approach from the southwest is reasonably straightforward. Further north rocks southwest of Gigalum only 0·3 and 0·6 metres high lie within 1½ cables of Gigha, but the most westerly of these is marked by a thin steel perch.

The pier is constructed of concrete piles, which are not convenient to lie alongside. There is no regular steamer service, but a boat should not be left unattended at the pier. The berth on the north side, with a depth of about 1·5 metres, is used for fuelling. A berth on the southwest side on the inner side of the head has a low-level landing platform and steps and the depth there also appears to be 1·5 metres.

In easterly winds some shelter may be found north of the 3-metre-high rock near the west side of Gigalum, but look out for a submerged rock between the 3-metre rock and the ferry mooring.

Supplies at Ardminish, except for diesel which is at this pier.

Ardminish

55°40′N 5°44′W

The most popular anchorage on Gigha, with HIDB visitors' moorings. Both points of the entrance are very foul; drying rocks extend a cable north of the most northerly rock above water at the south point, marked by an unlit red can buoy; submerged and drying rocks extend a cable southeast from the north point. The southwest side of the bay is shoal and

Caolas Gigalum from northeast. Gigalum is on the left and Eilean Leim, the south point of Gigha, at the top of the photo.

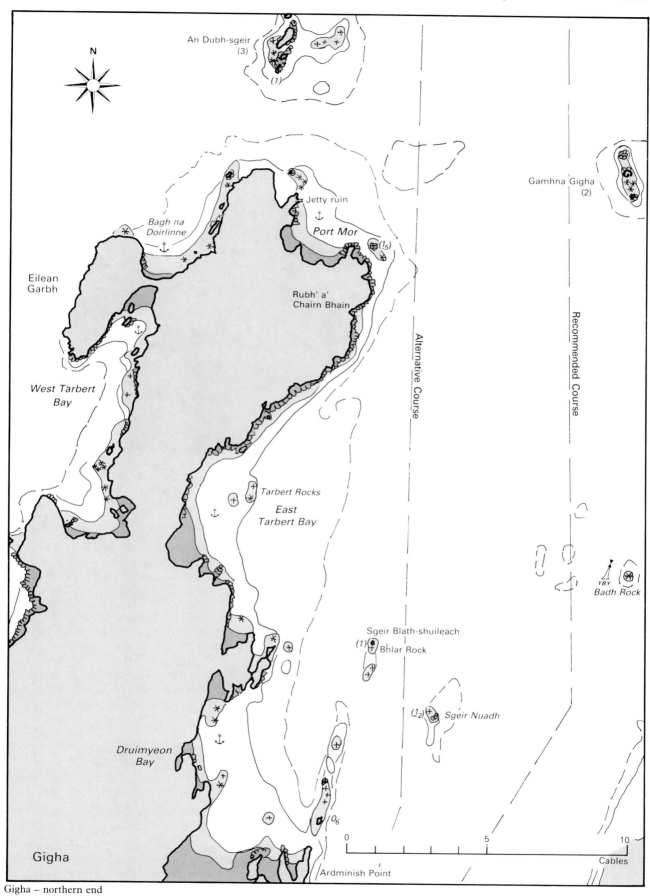

N

An Dubh-sgeir
(3)

(1)

Gamhna Gigha
(2)

Bagh na
Doirlinne

Jetty ruin

Port Mor

(1₅)

Eilean
Garbh

Rubh' a'
Chairn Bhain

Alternative Course

Recommended Course

*West Tarbert
Bay*

1

Tarbert Rocks

*East
Tarbert Bay*

YBY
Badh Rock

Sgeir Blath-shuileach

(1) Bhlar Rock

(1₂) *Sgeir Nuadh*

*Druimyeon
Bay*

0₆

Gigha

0   5   10

Ardminish Point

Cables

Gigha – northern end

Ardminish Bay from northeast.

Kiln Rock (Sgeir na h-Atho) dries 1·5 metres a cable ENE of the old ferry jetty at the middle of the west side of the bay.

Approach with the stone building at the old ferry jetty bearing 270° (not the car ferry slip at the northwest side of the bay), and anchor clear of Kiln Rock (which is usually showing) and clear of the approach to the car ferry slip.

Supplies

Shop and post office, telephone, hotel, *Calor Gas* at shop, water tap on east wall of the Boathouse tearoom (stone building by the old jetty); refuse disposal at Boathouse. Diesel at Caolas Gigalum pier; for small quantities (less than 11 litres) arrange with hotel, ☎ Gigha (058 35) 232; or for larger amounts, Gigha Engineering, ☎ Gigha (058 35) 261. Showers and baths at hotel.

Druimyeon Bay

55°41'·5N 5°43'W

More peaceful than Ardminish but not very convenient to find a way ashore. From the north approach by the northwest side of Bhlar Rock. From the south pass between Ardminish Point and Sgeir Mhor (0·6 metres high) which is ¾ cable from the point, but keep closer to Ardminish Point to avoid a rock spit extending south from Sgeir Mhor. There is a submerged rock with a depth of only 0·3m a cable offshore nearly 2 cables northwest of Ardminish Point, and drying rocks ½ cable northeast of Rubha Breac. Fish cages are moored west of Druimyeon Reef. Good anchorage close to the west shore north of Rubha Breac.

Occasional anchorages

East Tarbert Bay, avoiding Tarbert Rocks and shellfish floats in the middle of the bay.

Port Mor, at the north end of Gigha, and also in the small inlet northwest of Port Mor.

Eilean Garbh, 55°43'·5N 5°44'·5W, northwest of Gigha. In quiet weather either north or south of the shingle spit connecting Eilean Garbh to Gigha.

Port Mor at the north end of Gigha. Rocks extend further off the point on the left.

West Loch Tarbert

55°45′N 5°36′W

A rather narrow, pleasantly wooded loch, with many hazards on either side, but well marked as the ferry terminal for Islay is halfway up the loch; a pier at the head is extensively used by fishing boats. Fish cages and shellfish floats are moored off both shores throughout the loch.

Chart

2477 (1:25,000), OS map *62*

Tides

The in-going stream begins about +0430 Oban (−0100 Dover), and the out-going stream begins about −0200 Oban (+0500 Dover).

Constant is approximately −0200 Oban (+0500 Dover) at springs, −0500 Oban (+0300 Dover) at neaps.

Height in metres

MHWS	MHWN	MTL	MLWN	MLWS
1·5	1·3	1·0	0·8	0·6

Directions

The entrance is identified by a conspicuous conical hill Dun Skeig, 142 metres, on the south side of the entrance.

Approaching from north a light beacon (a steel column) must be identified 2 cables south of Eilean Traighe, a low island on the north side of the entrance.

Pass south of the Eilean Traighe beacon and north of Corran Point beacon, a mile further northeast 1½ cables off the south shore. For the next mile keep these two beacons in line astern to clear submerged and drying rocks 4 cables off the south shore.

Two further beacons at approximately 1½ mile intervals are passed, the first to port and the second to starboard. Kennacraig ferry terminal is ¾ mile further on the southeast shore, with a red light buoy ¼ mile northwest of it marking submerged and drying rocks which extend ½ mile from the northwest shore over a length of a mile.

Beyond Kennacraig the loch narrows and there are unmarked dangers, mostly on the north side. There are no beacons or buoys beyond Kennacraig.

The pier ¾ mile from the head of the loch is owned by Tarbert Fishermen's Association and is heavily used, particularly at weekends. Beyond the pier most of the loch dries.

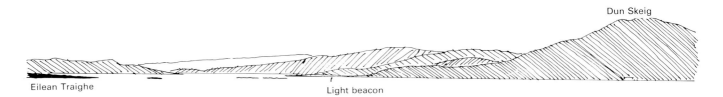

Dun Skeig

Eilean Traighe   Light beacon

West Loch Tarbert entrance.

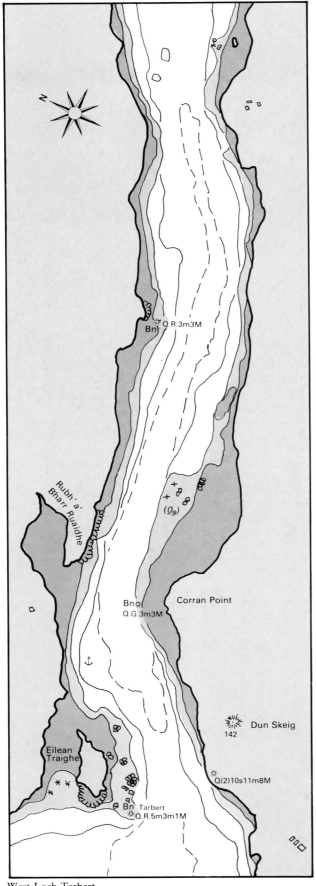

West Loch Tarbert

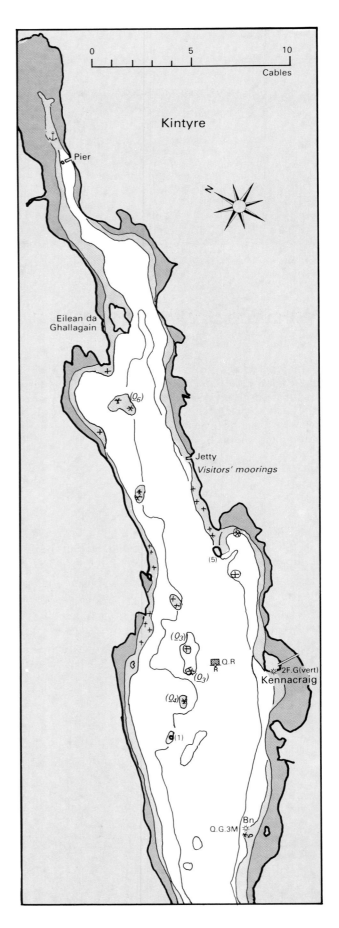

Head of West Loch Tarbert. The fishery pier is at the bottom left.

Anchorages and moorings

Northeast of Eilean Traighe, sand and weed. It is disturbed by wash from ferries and fishing boats, as is any part of the loch, but especially southwest of Kennacraig.

Moorings are available for visiting yachts off the jetty at Rhu House, about a mile northeast of Kennacraig ferry terminal. Call at Rhu House (West Tarbert Ventures, ☎ 08802 231) after picking up mooring.

Head of the loch, beyond the pier, closer to the southeast shore. Yachts should not be left unattended alongside the pier; you may come back to find six fishing boats rafted up outside you. Water at pier; supplies and services at Tarbert, 1½ miles from the pier (*see Chapter IV*).

Loch Stornoway provides an occasional anchorage in settled weather with a fine white sandy beach but is dramatically labelled 'dangerous' on the chart. Drying rocks extend a cable north of Sgeir Choigreach, the outer islet on the south side of the entrance, but George Jarvis says that Montgomerie Rocks on the north side seem to extend further south than shown and recommends keeping towards the islets. Clear out if any sea is coming in.

VI. South coast of Islay

The southeast side of Islay is an area rich in history: Dunyveg Castle at the entrance to Lagavulin Bay was the headquarters of the Lords of the Isles after the Norsemen were defeated at the Battle of Largs in 1263, and the finest carved medieval stone cross in Scotland is at Kildalton Chapel, near Port Mor and Glas Uig, north of Ardmore.

The inner passages between Ardmore and Port Ellen have been used by local fishermen and traders for centuries, but have only been brought to the notice of yachtsmen in the last few years by Michael Gilkes.

Chart

2168 (1:75,000), OS map *60*

Caution Chart *2168* is the only one published and is at quite an inadequate scale. The sketch plans here are based on Admiralty surveys of about 1860, together with air photographs and personal visits, but not a detailed recent survey.

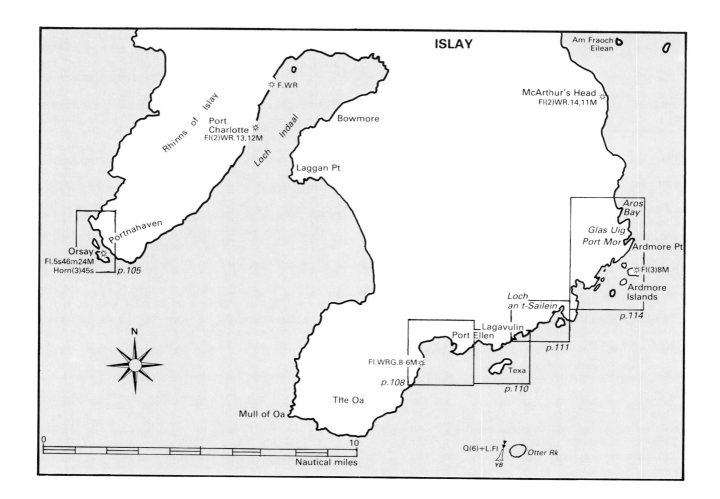

Tides

Between Islay and Kintyre and through the Sound of Jura as far as Fladda the rise and fall of tides is related to a phenomenon known as an amphidrome which is a tidal pivot point where the range is nil. This occurs about halfway between Port Ellen and the Mull of Kintyre, but its exact location moves during the tidal cycle; there is less range of tide on the southeast coast of Islay at the time of spring tides because the amphidrome is nearer to Islay at that time. This (rather simplified) is the reason for the curious observation in the Admiralty *Tide Tables* that 'it is neaps at Port Ellen when it is springs at Machrihanish'.

However there are strong tidal streams nearby, in particular at the Oa and the Rhinns of Islay, at the Mull of Kintyre, and in the Sound of Islay.

Off the Oa and the Rhinns the northwest-going stream begins about +0530 Oban (HW Dover) and the southeast-going stream begins about −0040 Oban (−0610 Dover). These streams reach a rate of 8 knots at springs off Orsay, Rhinns of Islay, and 5 knots off the Oa.

At Otter Rock the streams run east and west. The west-going stream begins as the northwest-going stream above, but the east-going stream begins ½ hour earlier than the southeast-going streams above.

Overfalls form off the southeast side of the Oa during northwest-going streams and off its southwest side during southeast-going streams.

Off Texa Island, tidal streams split, one stream running towards Ardmore, the other towards Rubha nan Leacan at the southeast point of the Oa beginning at about +0530 Oban (HW Dover), and running from those points towards Texa beginning about −0030 Oban (−0600 Dover).

Dangers and marks

Dangers and marks related to an extended coastal passage are described in sequence from Rhinns of Islay to Ardmore. Those related to individual anchorages and inshore passages will be described separately.

Off the Rhinns of Islay, Orsay island has a white lighthouse 46 metres high. A detached rock An Coire lies 1½ cables southwest of Orsay, round which very strong tidal streams run.

The Oa, the south point of Islay, which rises to 200 metres, has a tall stone monument at Mull of Oa, its southwest point.

Otter Rock, with a least depth of 3·7 metres, 3 miles south of Texa, is marked by a south cardinal light buoy.

Texa Island is 2 miles east of Port Ellen. Tarr Sgeir, a detached rock 4 metres high, lies 6 cables south of Texa and there are other rocks between Tarr Sgeir and Texa.

Iomallach, 2 metres high, 1¾ miles ENE of the northeast end of Texa and a mile south of Ard Imersay lies at the extremity of an area of rocks south and southwest of Ard Imersay. Ruadh Mor, 4 cables southwest of Iomallach has a depth of only 2·1 metres.

Ardmore Point is the most easterly point of Islay and Eilean a'Chuirn, nearly a mile south of Ardmore and 5 miles northeast of Texa, is the most easterly of the Ardmore Islands. Eilean a'Chuirn light beacon is an inconspicuous tower.

The Ardmore Islands run northeast from Ceann nan Sgeirean, 1 mile northeast of Ard Imersay, for 1½ miles and drying rocks lie up to 3 cables southeast of Ceann nan Sgeirean.

Passage notes to pass southwest of Islay

If conditions become unfavourable, Port Ellen is a convenient anchorage but tends to be subject to swell. Portnahaven, behind Orsay, provides good shelter but strong tides run across the entrance which can be difficult in deteriorating conditions.

Alternatively, the route by the Sound of Islay is no greater distance for a passage to the west of Mull, with more shelter and more anchorages on the way. Few yachts make a direct passage to the Outer Hebrides by way of Skerryvore, but even this passage is probably no further by the Sound of Islay. However, the outside passage is discussed below.

Because of overfalls, the Oa and the Rhinns of Islay should be passed at a distance of several miles (overfalls southwest of the Oa are worst with a southeast-going tide). As it is 36 miles from the Mull of Kintyre to the Rhinns of Islay only a fast boat under very favourable conditions could pass these two points in a single tide, and it is normally best to take a foul tide in the open water between Kintyre and Islay, aiming to be at the Oa at slack water.

There are more overfalls in unsettled weather over West Bank, 4 miles northwest of Orsay, as well as over banks six miles further NNW.

Dubh Artach lighthouse, which is distinguished by a broad red horizontal band, is 28 miles north of Orsay. Rocks above water and drying extend up to ½ mile southwest and northwest of the lighthouse so that it is best passed on its northeast side.

Skerryvore lighthouse, about 42 miles NNW from Orsay, has no red band. Several detached rocks lie up to 3 miles southwest of the lighthouse and there are strong tidal streams over relatively shoal water. The lighthouse should be passed at least 5 miles to the southwest in a depth of not less than 15 metres.

Lights

Rhinns of Islay (Orsay) Fl.5s46m24M
Rubha an Duin (Port Charlotte) Fl(2)WR.7s15m13/12M
Carraig Fhada (Port Ellen) Fl.WRG.3s19m9-6M
Otter Rock Q(6)+LFl.15s
Eilean a'Chuirn Fl(3)18s26m8M
Mull of Kintyre lighthouse Fl(2)20s91m29M
Altacarry Head Fl(4)20s74m26M
Rathlin West Fl.R.5s62m22M
Dubh Artach Fl(2)30s44m20M

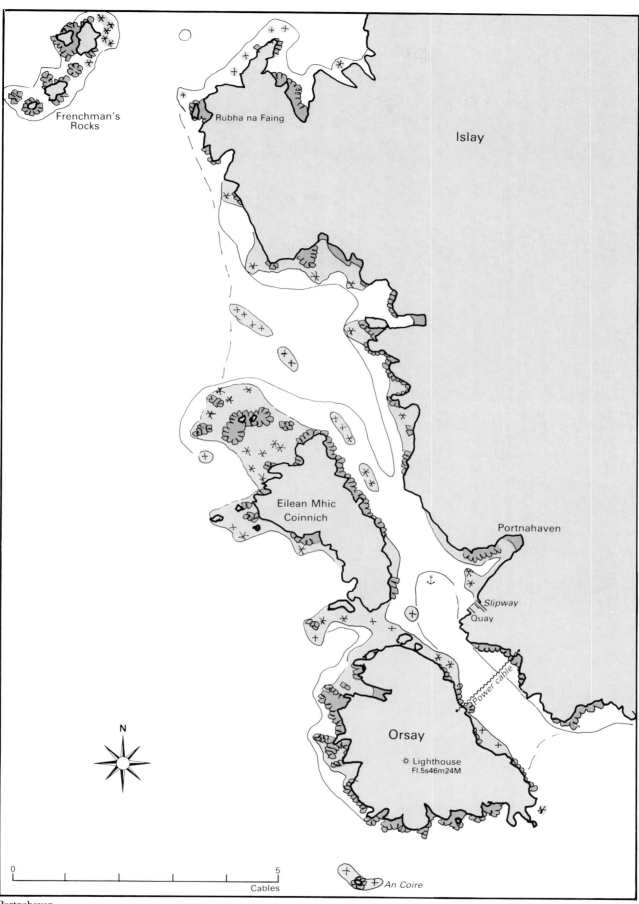

Frenchman's
Rocks

Rubha na Faing

Islay

Eilean Mhic
Coinnich

Portnahaven

⚓

✳ Slipway
Quay

Power cable

Orsay

✳ Lighthouse
Fl.5s46m24M

N

0   5
Cables

+ An Coire

Portnahaven

Orsay from southwest at springs; the tide is running strongly to
the northwest over An Coire.

Portnahaven from northwest. The quay and boatyard are at the
right.

Portnahaven

55°41'N 6°31'W

The channel between Orsay and the Rhinns of Islay is well sheltered with a sandy bottom, but strong tides run across the entrance.

Tides

Constant −0055 Oban (+0605 Dover)

Height in metres

MHWS	MHWN	MTL	MLWN	MLWS
2·6	2·3	1·7	1·3	0·5

Directions

The north entrance is obstructed by submerged rocks and should not be attempted.

Keep towards the Islay shore when approaching unless you are certain that the tide is running towards southeast to avoid being carried onto An Coire, southwest of Orsay. Anchor north of the quay on the Islay shore, where the channel opens out.

Small boats can use a creek on the Islay shore northeast of the quay, but the approach is intricate and the creek is often full of local fishing boats. Ian Wallace has provided the following directions: from southeast head for a white single-storey house on the shore on the northwest side of the entrance until about 20 metres from the shore. Weed on the reefs at the entrance is usually visible at any state of tide, and a passage a few metres wide through the weed leads diagonally to the opposite shore, towards a house in the terrace ahead which has a rectangular extension on the roof. Turn to head along the middle of the creek as soon as the reef to port is passed and drop your main anchor almost immediately. There are rings on either shore to which to take lines ashore.

Supplies

Shops, post office, telephone, hotel.

Loch Indaal

For passage notes and landmarks in the approach see the beginning of this chapter. Loch Indaal is a broad shallow loch whose interest is mainly in the several small towns and villages around it. Bowmore, the 'capital' of the island, has a distillery which provides guided tours. The Museum of Islay Life at Port Charlotte is worth visiting.

Chart

2168 (1:75,000)

Tides

Constant −0040 Oban (−0610 Dover)

Height in metres

MHWS	MHWN	MTL	MLWN	MLWS
2·3	1·5	1·5	1·4	0·8

Dangers and marks

Off Laggan Point, the east point of the entrance, submerged rocks extend WSW for ½ mile, and rocks above water extend up to ¼ mile from the southeast shore. Shellfish floats may be found ½ mile off the northwest shore.

The head of the loch dries for ¾ mile and the shores all round the head are shoal with drying patches.

Port Charlotte and Bruichladdich on the west shore are prominent; a white light beacon 13 metres high stands at Rubh'an Duin, ½ mile north of Port Charlotte.

Rubh'an Duin light beacon, Fl(2)WR.7s15m13/12M, shows white in the approach and in the upper part of the loch, and red over dangers near the east shore.

Anchorage

Occasional anchorage may be found off Port Charlotte.

A timber pier at Bruichladdich has a depth of 3 metres at its head. At night 2F.R(vert) lights are shown from the pier.

Supplies

Shops, post office, telephone, hotel, *Calor Gas*, petrol, diesel, water.

Bowmore

A small drying boat harbour is formed by a curved stone quay, but the 2-metre line is 2 cables offshore. A rock, and the end of a sewer outfall, 2 cables NNW of the quay are marked by a beacon. A beacon 2½ cables southwest of the first marks another rock. Anchor north of the north beacon.

Supplies

Shops, post office, bank, telephone, hotel; petrol and diesel at garage. *Calor Gas* at Bruichladdich.

Port Ellen

55°38'N 6°11'W

The main ferry terminal and harbour on Islay; for yachts better shelter will be found in Loch an t-Sailein (see below), although the approach is more difficult and there are no supplies.

Chart

Plan on *2474* (1:15,000)

Tides

Constant −0530 Oban (+0130 Dover) at springs, and −0050 Oban (+0610 Dover) at neaps.

Height in metres

MHWS	MHWN	MTL	MLWN	MLWS
0·9	0·8	0·6	0·5	0·3

Bowmore from north-northeast.

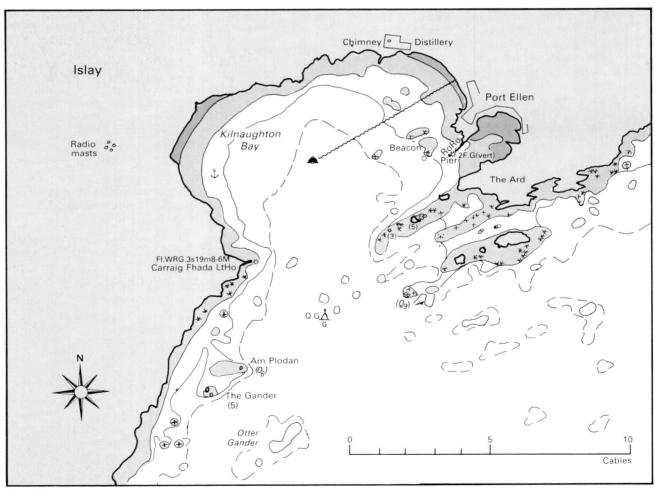

Port Ellen

Port Ellen approach. The lighthouse in line with the radio masts leads southeast of the buoy.

Port Ellen from northeast. Most of the bay in the foreground dries.

Dangers and marks

See also the passage notes at the beginning of this chapter particularly for Otter Rock and Tarr Sgeir.

Carraig Fhada lighthouse, a rectangular white tower, marks the west point of the bay.

The outer limit of submerged and drying reefs extending WSW from the east side of the bay is marked by a green conical light buoy 3 cables 130° from Carraig Fhada.

Rocks above water and submerged extend up to ¼ mile off the west shore SSW of Carraig Fhada. The Gander, 5 metres high, is 1½ cables offshore and ½ mile SSW of the lighthouse, and Am Plodan, 0·6 metres high, is 2½ cables offshore and 4 cables south of the lighthouse. Otter Gander, with a depth of 2·6 metres, is ½ mile offshore and 6 cables south of the lighthouse.

Port Ellen Pier on the east side of the bay has some shelter from the south behind a line of islets and skerries; Sgeir nan Ron a cable west of the pier is marked by a red beacon with a ball topmark. 2 cables west of this beacon is a submerged rock, and north of the beacon there are many submerged and drying rocks.

Approach

From southeast, pass south of Tarr Sgeir 6 cables south of Texa and steer towards Carraig Fhada lighthouse; the lighthouse in line with a group of radio masts on the hill above bearing 310° will lead to the green conical light buoy.

From southwest, if The Gander can be identified, and then Am Plodan, pass a cable east of these rocks. Otherwise keep a mile offshore and approach as from southeast to avoid Otter Gander.

Lights

Otter Rock light buoy Q(6)+LFl.15s
Carraig Fhada Fl.WRG.3s19m8-6M
The green conical light buoy Q.G
Port Ellen Pier head 2F.G(vert)

Anchorages

In westerly winds some shelter will be found in Kilnaughton Bay 4 cables NNW of the lighthouse.

At the pier anchor close north of the innermost islet south of the pier, clear of the approach to the pier which is used by ferries and by many fishing boats.

Perch

Approach to Port Ellen Pier.

Supplies

Shops, post office, telephone, hotels, *Calor Gas*, petrol, diesel at garage, water tap at pierhead.

Caolas an Eilean

This passage, between Texa and Islay, is 4 cables wide but there are rocks above and below water on the Islay side and a submerged rock a cable west of Texa, 2 cables south of a line from the north point of Texa to Port Ellen green buoy. At the east end of the passage continue ENE until Lagavulin bears 360°.

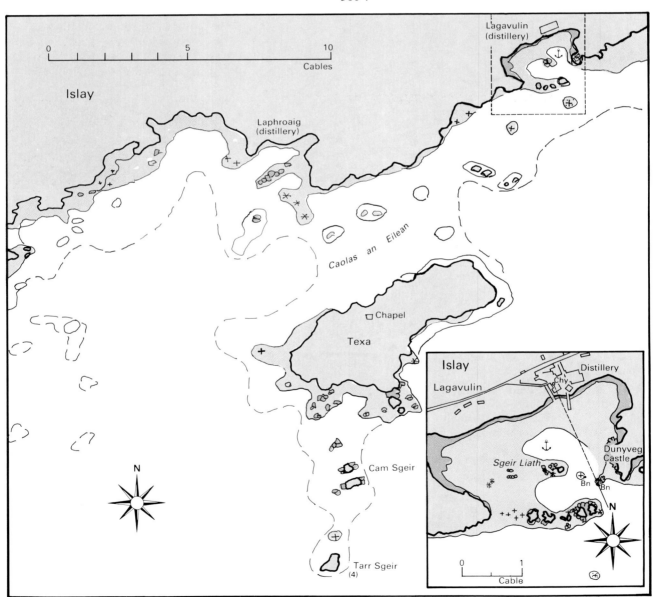

Passage between Texa and Islay

Lagavulin Bay and Loch an t-Sailean

55°38′N 6°07′W

Loch an t-Sailein provides better shelter than Lagavulin in most onshore winds. Two distilleries will be seen, Lagavulin, and Ardbeg which is ¾ mile further northeast.

Tides (at Port Ellen)

Constant −0530 Oban (+0130 Dover) at springs, and −0050 Oban (+0610 Dover) at neaps.

Height in metres

MHWS	MHWN	MTL	MLWN	MLWS
0·9	0·8	0·6	0·5	0·3

Dangers

Rocks above and below water extend over a mile south and southwest from Ard Imersay, which separates Loch an t-Sailein from Loch a'Chnuic. Iomallach, 2 metres high, is the outermost of these rocks above water. Submerged rocks extend 50 metres southwest from Iomallach, and Ruadh Mor, 4 cables southwest of Iomallach has a depth of 2·1 metres over it.

Approach

From east or northeast pass a cable south of Iomallach and steer west with the north point of Texa Island in line with Carraig Fhada lighthouse at Port Ellen. This course takes you over a rock with a depth of 3·4 metres.

On the starboard bow the name 'Lagavulin' painted on a warehouse at the distillery will appear from behind high ground, and begin to disappear behind Dunyveg Castle. Alter course towards the warehouse, keeping not more than the letters ULIN visible until the beacons in Lagavulin Bay to the left of the castle come into line.

From southeast steer with Lagavulin distillery (taking care not to mistake Ardbeg for it) bearing 315° to pass clear southwest of Ruadh Mor; bring the letters ULIN into sight and steer as above.

From southwest keep at least a cable off the east end of Texa and steer northeast until Lagavulin bears 360°. Before the rocks in the mouth of the bay are within two cables alter course to starboard to

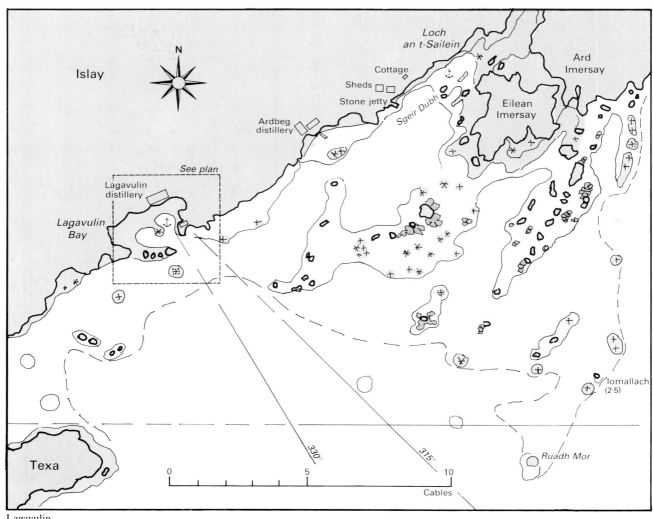

Lagavulin

bring the distillery into the gap between Gille na
Fead and Dunyveg Castle to avoid a rock awash a
cable south of Gille na Fead.

Carraig Fhada lighthouse just open north of Texa Island.

Iomallach. Texa on the left, Carraig Fhada lighthouse beyond.

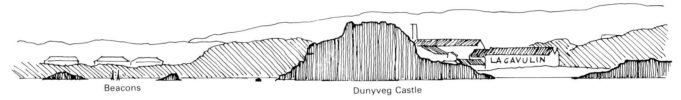

Approach to Lagavulin.

Loch an t-Sailein from northwest. The stone jetty is at the bottom right-hand corner.

To make for Loch an t-Sailein turn to starboard as soon as the Lagavulin beacons come into line, to avoid submerged rocks inshore, and steer parallel to the shore. Rocks above water will be seen ahead, SSW of Ardbeg distillery, with the remains of an iron beacon, and other rocks cover at HW about a cable south of these. Pass the above-water rocks on either hand and continue past a stone pier, and a white cottage to port, and Sgeir Dubh to starboard. Anchor north of Sgeir Dubh, avoiding a rocky shelf off the Islay shore.

If making for Lagavulin, alter course to port to keep the Lagavulin distillery chimney in line with the right-hand beacon. Steer to leave the first beacon to starboard and the second to port, passing between them and keeping rather closer to the second.

Anchorage and moorings – Lagavulin

Anchor north or northwest of Sgeir Liath in the middle of the bay, in about 2 metres. Mooring rings are fixed at the east and west ends of Sgeir Liath, and the distillery has laid two visitors' moorings marked LAG 1 and LAG 2 at the east side of the bay. There is 1·2 metre at the head of the pier, and 1·5 metre on its west side and it may be used by yachts (at owner's risk).

Water is available, and tours of the distillery arranged, at the visitor centre.

Lagavulin Bay from north-northwest.

Passage inshore of Ardmore Islands

55°40′N 6°02′W

The features of this passage are not easy to distinguish and it should only be attempted for the first time in clear quiet weather. The description must be read with the plan.

Tides (at Port Ellen)

Constant −0530 Oban (+0130 Dover) at springs, and −0050 Oban (+0610 Dover) at neaps.

Height in metres

MHWS	MHWN	MTL	MLWN	MLWS
0·9	0·8	0·6	0·5	0·3

Dangers and marks

The passage between Eilean Craobhach and Islay is known as Caolas Port na Lice. There are several lines of rocks on the southeast side of the passage of which the nearest may cover at a high spring tide. A shoal patch in the middle of the passage appears to be not less than 3 metres deep.

In the passage southwest of Eilean Craobhach the principal hazard is a rock awash in the middle of the basin 3 cables southwest of Eilean Craobhach; drying rocks 2 cables further SSW and 2 cables

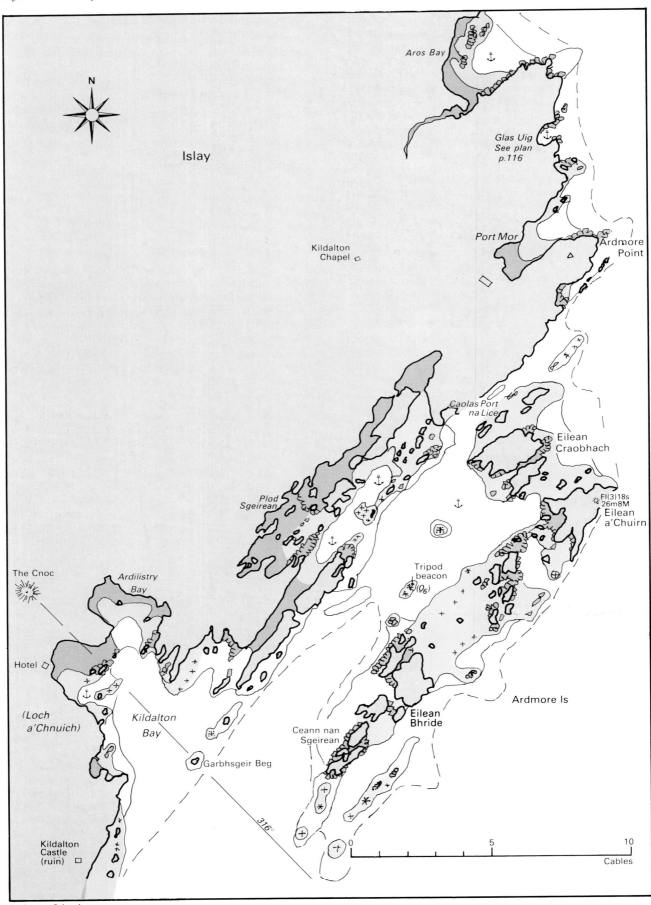

Islay

Aros Bay

*Glas Uig
See plan
p.116*

Port Mor

Ardmore
Point

Kildalton
Chapel

*Caolas Port
na Lice*

Eilean
Craobhach

*Plod
Sgeirean*

Fl(3)18s
26m8M
Eilean
a'Chuirn

The Cnoc

*Ardilistry
Bay*

Tripod
beacon
(Q₆)

Hotel

Ardmore Is

*(Loch
a'Chnuich)*

*Kildalton
Bay*

Ceann nan
Sgeirean

Eilean
Bhride

Garbhsgeir Beg

316°

Kildalton
Castle
(ruin)

0   5   10

Cables

Caolas Port na Lice from northeast.

From northeast keep ½ cable from the southeast side of Ardmore Point to pass inside the line of rocks north of Eilean Craobhach (not inshore of a line of rocks which are within about 20 metres of Ardmore). Keep about a cable off Plod Sgeirean, the line of skerries across the mouth of the rocky bay to starboard, until the tripod is in line with the east point of Eilean Bhride, and alter course to pass west of Ceann nan Sgeirean. Keep Garbh-sgeir Beg in line with the conical hill Cnoc Rhaonastil (The Cnoc) 316° astern or southwest of this line to avoid drying rocks south of Ceann nan Sgeirean.

Anchorages

Eilean Craobhach, 1½ cables off the southwest shore of the island, avoiding the rock awash.

Plod Sgeirean: Enter between the islet which forms the south point of the bay and the first skerry to the northeast, keeping rather nearer to the skerry. If anchoring at the south end turn to port when the channel opens out and anchor as far south as depth allows. To anchor at the north end keep heading towards the shore and turn to starboard when closer to the islet ahead than to the skerry in the entrance as there are submerged reefs northwest of the skerry.

Kildalton Bay (Loch a'Chnuic) is convenient for the hotel but subject to swell in easterly winds. Pass either side of Garbhsgeir Beg, but if on its north side not more than a cable away, and head towards Ardilistry Bay. There are two detached rocks off the southwest shore and then a rocky islet off the promontory which separates Ardilistry Bay from Kildalton Bay (Loch a'Chnuic); when this islet is almost abeam turn to port to pass southeast of it to avoid a reef extending northeast from the second detached rock. Anchor near the southwest shore at the mouth of Kildalton Bay.

north of Eilean Bhride are marked by a tripod beacon; a shoal spit lies between 2 and 4 cables WSW of the tripod beacon, with charted depths of 2–3 metres. Drying rocks extend to 3 cables south of Ceann nan Sgeirean, the southwest end of Ardmore Islands.

Directions

From south or southwest pass east of Iomallach, head NNE to pass northwest of Ardmore Islands and continue as below.

From southeast, the detached islet Garbhsgeir Beg in line with the conical hill Cnoc Rhaonastil (The Cnoc) 316° leads close southwest of drying rocks south of Ceann nan Sgeirean. When Ceann nan Sgeirean is aft of the beam steer to pass northwest of the tripod beacon. There is no clear mark to avoid the rock awash in the middle of the basin, but its west side should be cleared by keeping the tripod beacon in line with the east point of Eilean Bhride. Steer on this line to within a cable of the skerries at Plod Sgeirean and head for Caolas Port na Lice.

Anchorages north of Ardmore Point
See plan page 116

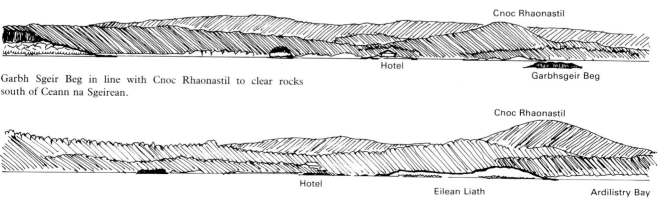

Garbh Sgeir Beg in line with Cnoc Rhaonastil to clear rocks south of Ceann na Sgeirean.

Approach to Loch a'Chnuich.

Loch a'Chnuich from west.

Tides (at Port Ellen)

Constant −0530 Oban (+0130 Dover) at springs, and −0050 Oban (+0610 Dover) at neaps.

Height in metres

MHWS	MHWN	MTL	MLWN	MLWS
0·9	0·8	0·6	0·5	0·3

Three open bays provide occasional anchorage north of Ardmore Point. These bays are all difficult to identify from seaward, but Ardmore Point has a triangulation point (a short tapering concrete pillar) near its summit and Port Mor has a large white house at its head.

Port Mor is immediately northwest of Ardmore Point. The head of the bay shoals a long way and there is a line of rocks on the northwest side of the bay. The bottom is clean sand.

Glas Uig is very difficult to distinguish and scarcely shows on chart *2168*; it is about 3 cables north of Port Mor. Anchor on the north side of the bay to avoid the submerged reef off the quay on the south side.

Aros Bay is a clean open sandy bay ¾ mile north of Ardmore Point; a pleasant place to spend a fine, windless day.

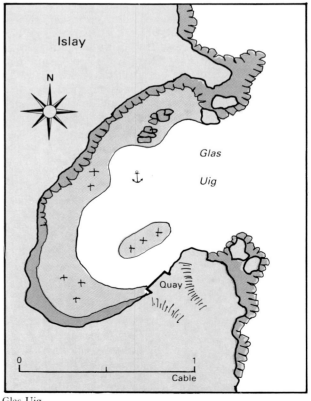

Glas Uig

Plod Sgeirean from west.

Glas Uig from the north shore.

Aros Bay from southwest.

VII. Sound of Islay and Colonsay

Charts

2168 includes the Sound of Islay and Loch Tarbert at 1:75,000; *2169* continues north at the same scale. *2481* covers the Sound of Islay and Loch Tarbert at 1:25,000.

Tidal streams

Tidal streams in the Sound of Islay run at up to 5 knots with eddies inshore.

The north-going stream begins about +0440 Oban (−0050 Dover), and the south-going stream begins about −0140 Oban (+0515 Dover).

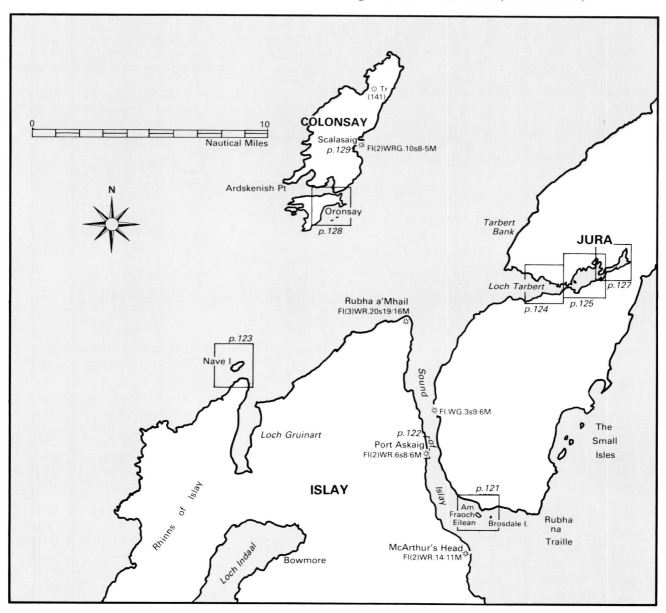

Overfalls form at the north end of the sound on the flood with a northerly wind, and at the south end of the sound on the ebb, where it meets the ebb from the Sound of Jura.

Dangers and marks

The main dangers are the Black Rocks near the south end of the sound, marked on their southwest side by a G conical light buoy. From either direction this buoy is likely to appear nearer to the Islay shore than might be expected.

Brosdale Island, south of Jura and east of the south end of the sound, has a submerged rock 3 cables south of its southwest side, and Am Fraoch Eilean, 1½ miles west of Brosdale Island, has rocks drying 1½ cables south of it.

At the north end of the sound Sgeir Traigh dries 3·6 metres 4 cables off the shore of Jura 2¾ miles north of Carragh an t-Sruith. Other rocks dry up to ¼ mile offshore for two miles further northeast. These rocks are dangerous, especially if tacking or making for Loch Tarbert, although Sgeir Traigh rarely completely covers. There are few distinguishing marks on Jura, but a prominent rocky streak Sgriob na Caillich (the Witch's Scratch) runs down the hillside to a point about ½ mile northeast of Sgeir Traigh.

Throughout the sound rocks both submerged and drying lie up to a cable from both shores.

For dangers beyond the north end of the sound see page 123.

To the west of the north end of the sound, Post Rocks dry up to 3·3 metres (they rarely cover), 1½ miles WNW of Rubha a'Mhail lighthouse, up to 7 cables offshore.

Conspicuous marks are, from south to north:

McArthur's Head lighthouse, a 13-metre white tower surrounded by a white-painted wall on a steep hillside on Islay south of the entrance to the sound.

Am Fraoich Eilean, off the Jura shore north of McArthur's Head.

Brosdale Island, 1½ miles further east.

Port Askaig village, 5 miles NNW of McArthur's Head.

Caol Ila distillery, ½ mile north of Port Askaig.

Bunnahabhainn (Bunnahaven) distillery, 2 miles north of Port Askaig.

Rubha a'Mhail (Ruvaal) lighthouse, 45 metres high, at the west point of the north end of the sound, about 3½ miles from Bunnahabhainn.

Lights

McArthur's Head lighthouse, Fl(2)WR.10s39m14/11M, shows white in Sound of Islay from the northeast coast of Islay to 159°-R-244°-W to the east coast of Islay

Black Rocks light buoy Q.G

Carraig Mor light beacon Fl(2)WR.6s7m8/6M; Islay shore-R-175°-W-347°-R-Islay

Carraig an t-Sruith light beacon Fl.WG.3s8m9/6M 354°-W-078°-G-170°-W-185°

Rubha a'Mhail lighthouse Fl(3)WR.15s45m24/21M 075°-R-180°-W-075

Directions

A passage east and north of the Black Rocks can be used to avoid an adverse tide in the south part of the sound. Approaching from southeast keep at least ¼ mile south of Am Fraoch Eilean; keep the green conical buoy bearing not less than 290°. Identify an isolated cottage on Jura and Sgeir nan Sian, and steer 360° for a rocky bluff between them; as a check on position the boathouse at Am Far Eilean will show up north of Am Fraoch Eilean soon after you turn onto this line. When Brosdale Island passes behind Am Far Eilean alter course to bring the south fall of Brosdale Island over the boathouse 112° astern to pass between Macphaill Rock and drying reefs on the Jura shore.

To make this passage from northwest to southeast, identify Am Far Eilean and Brosdale Island while passing Glas Eilean and reverse the directions given above.

For the passage from the Sound of Islay to Colonsay, and past Colonsay to Mull and to Tiree, see page 130.

Tides (at Port Askaig)

Constant −0030 Oban (+0500 Dover) at springs, and −0110 Oban (+0420 Dover) at neaps.

Height in metres
At Port Askaig

MHWS	MHWN	MTL	MLWN	MLWS
2·1	1·5	1·2	1·0	0·4

At Rubha a'Mhail

3·7	2·8	2·1	1·5	0·6

Note the difference in range in only 6 miles.

Anchorages

Am Far Eilean provides occasional anchorage north of Am Fraoch Eilean and southwest of the boathouse, in 3 metres.

Port Askaig has a temporary berth alongside a well fendered concrete quay. Eddies close inshore make the approach difficult. Alternatively anchor off the quay in 4 metres, clear of the approach to the quay, but the tide runs strongly here.

Check immediately on berthing that a car ferry is not due to arrive before you intend to leave; it is usually possible to stay overnight (dues charged). Moor towards the south end of the main ferry berth for shelter from the tide. A smaller ferry crosses frequently to Jura from a separate berth at the south end of the quay.

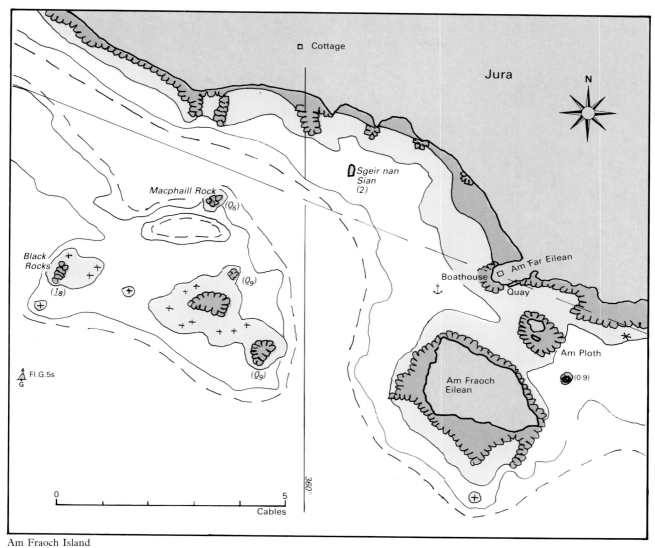

Am Fraoch Island

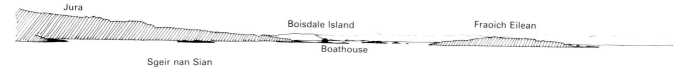

Am Far Eilean under the right fall of Brosdale leads north of
Macphaill Rock.

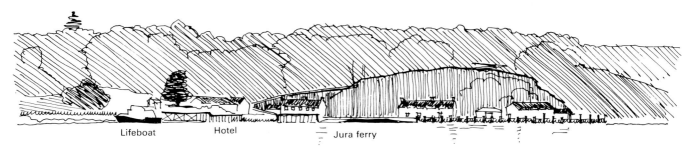

Port Askaig from east.

Port Askaig quay from south.

Port Askaig from northwest. A small yacht is moored between the two ferry berths, which seems a vulnerable position.

Supplies

Shop, post office, phone, water by hose, hotel, *Calor Gas*, petrol. Ferries to Jura and to mainland. Bus to Bowmore and Port Ellen.

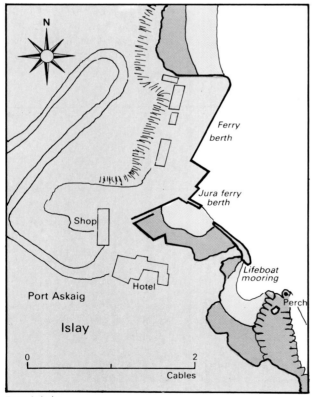

Port Askaig

Occasional anchorages

Caol Ila distillery: it may be possible to moor at the pier but it is used by local fishing boats; check that access will not be needed.

Whitefarland Bay, Jura, out of the main tidal stream opposite Caol Ila. Anchor off a boulder on which an anchor is painted in white. The bottom is weedy and holding poor. There is a mooring ring on shore close south of the white mark.

Bunnahaven is a convenient place to wait for a south-going tide; anchor north of the pier.

Northwest coast of Islay

Two groups of drying rocks lie off the northwest coast of Islay, Post Rocks, 1½ miles west of Rubha a'Mhail lighthouse at the north entrance to the Sound of Islay, and Balach Rocks, up to 2 miles northeast of Nave Island. A clearing mark for Post Rocks is the highest of the Paps of Jura in line with Rubha a'Mhail lighthouse 117°.

Occasional anchorage southeast of the middle of Nave Island; drying rocks fill the south end of the channel. Approach either from the north of Post Rocks, or round the northeast end of Nave Island, keeping ¼ mile off to avoid a reef at the end of the island and the innermost of the Balach Rocks.

Loch Gruinart is inaccessible to any except the most adventurous owners of shoal-draught boats prepared to explore with almost no information. The original Admiralty survey shows the sands at the mouth of the loch as quicksand.

Nave Island from east. Ardnave Point is on the extreme left.

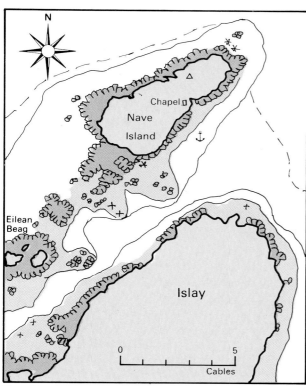

Nave Island

Loch Tarbert, Jura

Possibly the most remote loch in the Inner Hebrides in that it has no road access and is far from any other anchorage. The loch is littered with reefs but it has been well marked with leading beacons by the late H. G. Hasler.

Tides

Constant at Scalasaig (Colonsay) −0012 Oban (+0542 Dover).

Height in metres

MHWS	MHWN	MTL	MLWN	MLWS
3·9	2·7	2·2	1·6	0·5

Dangers and marks

The outer part of the loch has fewer hazards than the inner. Bo Mor, a submerged rock with a depth of 1·9 metres, lies 4 cables south of Rubh' an t-Sailein, the north point of the entrance. Eileanan Gleann Righ extend 3 cables from the north shore with drying rocks on their west side but the south and southeast sides are clean.

Off the mouth of Glenbatrick on the south shore opposite Eileanan Gleann Righ a reef Sgeir Agleann extends ½ mile northwards. A submerged rock at its outer end lies 2½ cables NNE from the outermost rock above water.

In southerly winds violent squalls spread out from Glenbatrick to cause confusion, just when the navigational hazards need all your concentration.

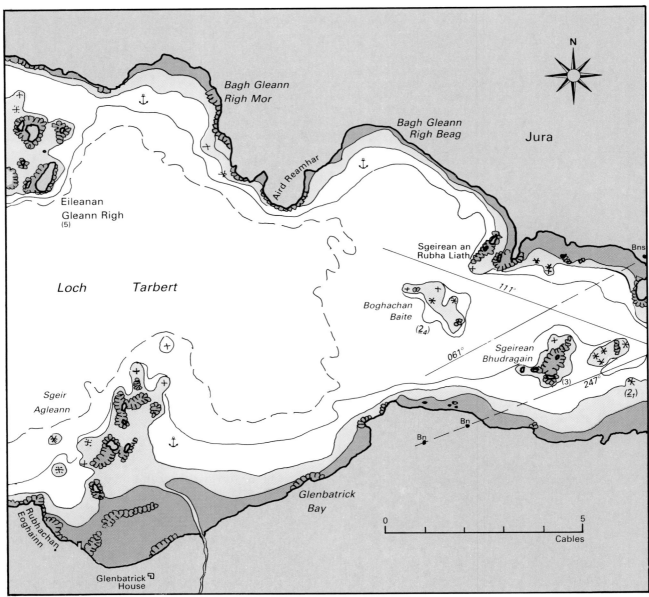

Loch Tarbert

Anchorages in the outer loch

Glenbatrick Bay provides some shelter on the east side of Sgeir Agleann but the shore dries off 2 cables at the mouth of the river.

Three bays on the north side of the loch provide occasional anchorage:

An Sailein, 4 cables east of Rubh' an t-Sailein; note drying rocks more than a cable west of Eileanan Gleann Righ.

Bagh Gleann Righ Mor, ENE of Eileanan Gleann Righ. There is over 3 metres depth north of the islands but the passage through is blocked by rocks at its west end.

Bagh Gleann Righ Beag, east of Aird Reamhar, which is 6 cables east of Eileanan Gleann Righ.

Passage to the inner loch

Boghachan Baite, 8 cables ENE of Sgeir Agleann is a large area of rocks drying up to 2·4 metres, where the cleaner passage is on the south side. Sgeirean Bhudragain, 3 cables further ESE, is another patch of rocks, up to 3 metres high with extensive drying areas, where the cleaner passage is on the north side.

A pair of concrete beacons on the north shore in line about 061° lead southeast of Boghachan Baite; another pair on the southeast shore in line about 111° leads north of Sgeirean Bhudragain (and also north of Boghachan Baite if you prefer to go that way).

A further set of beacons on the south shore about 247° (astern when entering) lead south of Sgeirean Bhudragain, but this is a trickier passage used

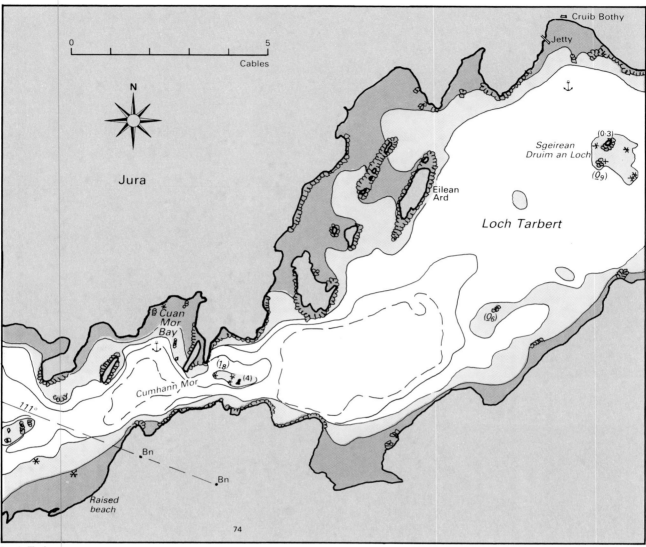

Loch Tarbert

mainly by shoal-draught estate motor launches. A detached drying rock on the southeast side of this line may be marked by a small white buoy.

The most popular anchorage is in Cuan Mor Bay northwest of Cumhann Mor, 6 cables ENE of Sgeirean Bhudragain. A drying reef lies on the east side of the bay and two cairns in line on the hillside north of the bay lead close west of it. The head of the bay dries for at least a cable.

From Sgeirean Bhudragain the loch is clean to the narrows of Cumhann (Cuan) Mor, after which the passage to the inner loch is south of an islet 4 metres high. At first the inner loch is very deep, but after half a mile most of it is less than 3 metres deep with patches of less than 2 metres depth. A rock dries 0·6 metres 2 cables off the south shore 8 cables ENE of Cumhann Mor. Sgeirean Druim an Loch, a patch of rocks the highest of which is 0·3 metres above high water, lies towards the head of the loch 1¼ miles northeast of Cumhann Mor.

After passing south of the 4-metre islet east of Cumhann Mor, head northeast to follow that shore until Sgeirean Druim an Loch is identified. The

cottage north of Sgeirean Druim an Loch (Cruib Bothy) is reported to be ruined. The inner loch is shoal on all sides so that it is necessary except for shallow-draught boats, or at neaps, to anchor well offshore; the anchorage off Cruib Bothy is well spoken of, but note that drying rocks lie a cable offshore in the middle of the bay.

Cumhann Beag

55°58′N 5°53′W

Towards the head of the inner loch Cumhann Beag leads to an intricate series of narrow rocky channels which in turn lead to a shallow basin which is only ¾ mile from the east coast of Jura. Unless you can be sure of the position of the drying rock off the south shore and the most southerly rock of Sgeirean Druim an Loch (sometimes marked by a small white buoy), it is best to approach by the north of Sgeirean Druim an Loch; but if, after passing northeast of Cumhann Mor, the 247° leading beacons can still be clearly seen astern, they should lead clear of these rocks to Cumhann Beag.

Loch Tarbert, Jura. Cumhann Beag from southwest.

Loch Tarbert, Jura. Entrance to Cumhann Beag channels, from
south.

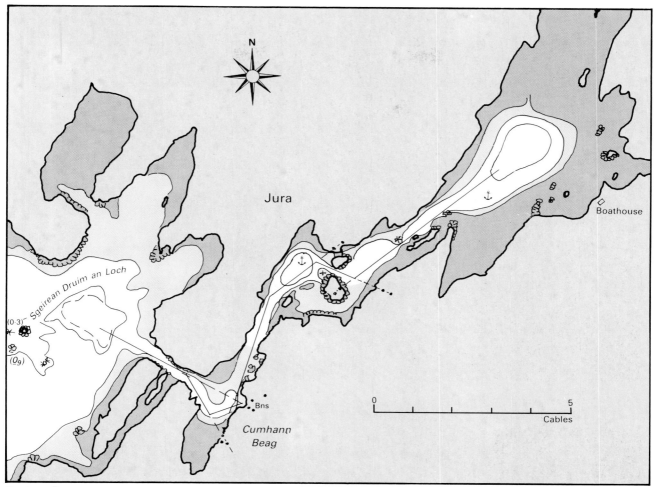

Cumhann Beag

Colonsay and Oronsay

Charts

2169 (1:75,000) is the only current chart for Colonsay, but an old chart *2418* (1:24,430) with depths in fathoms shows the island in great detail. OS map *61*.

Tides (at Scalasaig)

Constant −0012 Oban (+0542 Dover)

Height in metres

MHWS	MHWN	MTL	MLWN	MLWS
3·9	2·7	2·2	1·6	0·5

Marks

From northeast there is little to distinguish any part of the island, but from the north end of the Sound of Islay Beinn Oronsay (91 metres) shows up as a wedge-shaped hill with a sheer cliff on its south side.

Closer to Colonsay a monument on the skyline between Scalasaig and Loch Staosnaig is the best mark; the lighthouse south of Scalasaig is a low white rectangular building.

The tide runs strongly in Cumhann Beag so that the stream gives the impression of running downhill. A further series of marks, smaller than the beacons in the outer loch will, if followed precisely, lead through these channels but they are best taken at slack water.

The first four pairs of marks are close together. The first is straight ahead on entering and the second leads to starboard to avoid a sandbank on the inside of a sharp turn to port. The third pair leads to port and the fourth pair is astern (the front mark of the fourth pair has fallen over and is at about HW level). The fifth pair is ½ mile ahead to starboard and the sixth leads sharp to starboard between two islands. The seventh pair is astern and needs to be particularly carefully followed as the dangers which it clears are 2–3 cables from the marks.

The basin dries on all sides, especially at the head; anchor wherever there is enough depth and swinging room. Good anchorage has also been found in the bay WSW of the fifth pair of marks. A track from a boathouse on the east side of the basin leads to the road at Tarbert Bay on the east side of Jura.

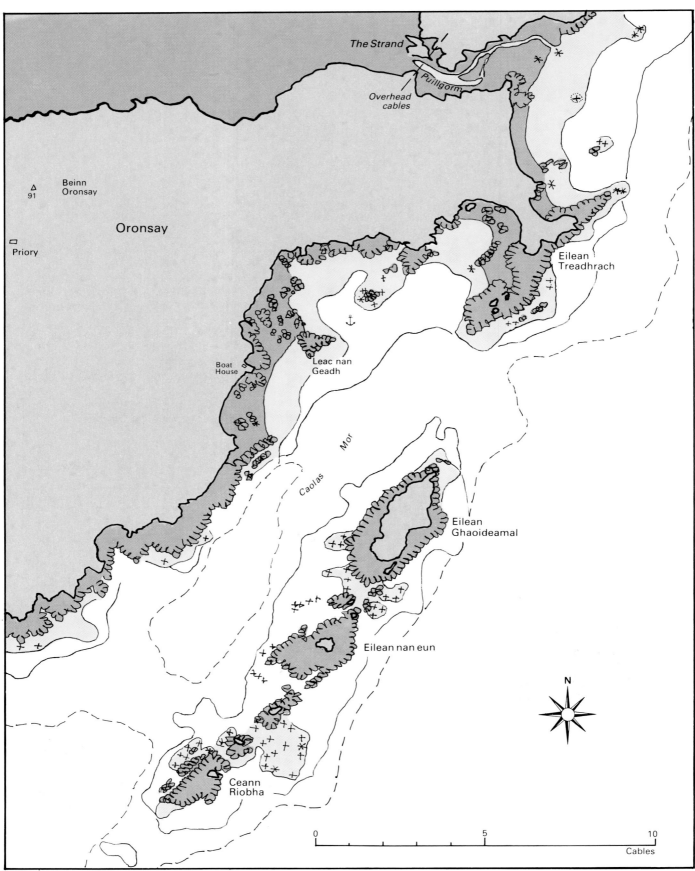

The Strand

Puillgorm

Overhead cables

△ Beinn
91 Oronsay

Oronsay

◻ Priory

Eilean
Treadhrach

⚓

Boat
House

Leac nan
Geadh

Caolas Mor

Caolas

Eilean
Ghaoideamal

Eilean nan eun

N

Ceann
Riobha

0   5   10
Cables

Caolas Mor

Caolas Mor, Oronsay

56°01′N 6°13′W

Occasional anchorage in the sound between Oronsay and the islands southeast of it.

Approaching from the Sound of Islay pass ¼ mile north of Eilean Ghaoideamal and anchor off the boathouse, taking care to avoid the reef Leac nan Geadh which covers.

Coming from northeast steer towards Eilean Ghaoideamal until the boathouse bears 270° and then steer to keep it on that bearing.

If Leac nan Geadh is identified better shelter can be found a cable north of it. The bight inside the peninsula Eilean Treadhrach is sometimes preferred, and in southwesterly winds a better berth may be found on the north side of Eilean Treadhrach.

Oronsay Priory is about a mile from the boathouse.

Loch Staosnaig

56°03′·5N 6°11′W

The monument on the skyline north of the bay is a good landmark for initial identification. Anchor near the head of the bay towards its south side to avoid power cables which come ashore north of Eilean Scalasaig. Two beacons in line show the approximate line of the cable. As at Scalasaig subject to swell, but with more space.

Scalasaig

56°04′N 6°11′W

Charts

Plan on *2474* (1:12,500), *2169* (1:75,000)

Tides

Constant −0012 Oban (+0542 Dover)

Height in metres

MHWS	MHWN	MTL	MLWN	MLWS
3·9	2·7	2·2	1·6	0·5

Directions

Even in westerly winds a swell usually works into Scalasaig and there is very little swinging room. On approaching from southward there is little sign of the village until it bears 270°, and the first mark to be seen is the monument on the skyline. A linkspan for a car ferry has been built on the south side of the pier.

There is no room for yachts to anchor clear of the ferry terminal on the south side of the pier, and the bottom has been dredged down to bare rock. A wave screen of timber boarding is to be constructed near the root of the north side of the pier for visiting yachts to lie alongside. Fishing boats often congregate on the north side of the pier overnight.

Supplies

Small shop, post office, phone, hotel, *Calor Gas*, bicycle hire at hotel.

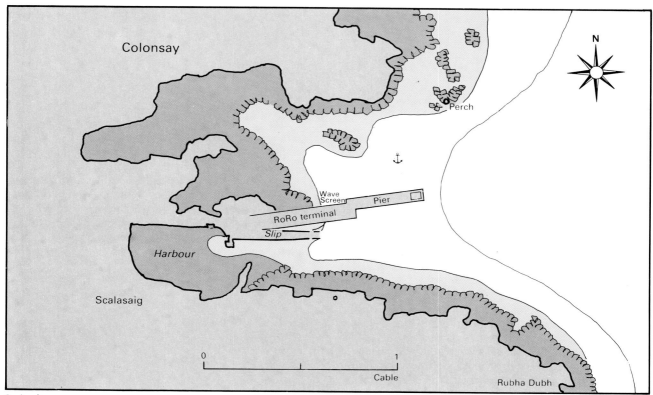

Scalasaig

Scalasaig from southeast (before construction of RoRo terminal).

Scalasaig approach from northeast.

Passages past Colonsay to Mull and Tiree

The passage from the Sound of Islay past the east side of Colonsay is straightforward. In good visibility from a point 1 mile northeast of Colonsay steer 330° towards the highest point of the Ross of Mull, Beinn a Chaol-achadh, and the nearest point on the shore there, Rubh' Ardalanish, a distance of about 8 miles. Directions for the passage between the Torran Rocks and Mull are given in the companion volume, *Crinan to Canna*.

In the passage south of Colonsay, there are two main hazards, the Post Rocks 1½ miles west of Rubha a'Mhail lighthouse, and Bogha Chubaidth awash 1½ miles southwest of Oronsay. Rubha a'Mhail lighthouse in line with Beinn an Oir, the highest, and from this direction the central hill of the Paps of Jura, bearing 117° leads well north of Post Rocks, and the lighthouse in line with Beinn Shiantaidh the more northerly of the Paps bearing 112° leads well south of Bogha Chubaidth.

Once clear west of Oronsay steer 315° to pass northeast of Dubh Artach lighthouse which is distinguished by a broad red band painted round it. Tiree is low-lying but has two hills in its western part, Ben Hynish and Ben Hough, which in clear weather will be the first part of Tiree to be seen.

For the passage south of Tiree see the beginning of Chapter VI, and for the passage through Gunna Sound see *Crinan to Canna*.

VIII. Sound of Jura

The Gaelic dictionary which I use gives as an alternative name for the Sound of Jura 'an linne rosach' (the channel of disappointment) because of the strong tides and the awkward seas raised by the wind against tide and the uneven bottom. The seas are at their worst when the wind is southerly, blowing from the open sea against an ebb tide, but eddies on the flood can be just as troublesome.

Charts

2168, 2169 (1:75,000) each include part of the sound. Much greater detail is provided by *2396* and *2397* at 1:25,000.

Tides

Throughout the sound most of the rise and fall occurs within the first three hours of each period. The height of tide is greatly affected by wind and barometric pressure; a southwesterly wind and/or low pressure raising the level by up to a metre, and a northeasterly wind and/or high pressure reducing it by a similar amount.

Throughout the greater part of the sound the north-going stream begins about +0545 Oban (+0015 Dover) and the south-going stream begins about −0015 Oban (−0545 Dover). The rate at the south end of the sound is about 2 knots, and around Skervuile about 3–3½ knots.

Near Ruadh Sgeir at the north end of the sound the north-going stream begins about +0425 Oban (−0105 Dover) and the south-going stream begins about −0155 Oban (+0500 Dover), the rate in each direction being up to 4 knots.

Conspicuous marks

The Paps of Jura, a group of three conspicuous hills near the south end of Jura, provide a useful reference point unless they are obscured by cloud.

Na Cuiltean, a rock east of the south end of Jura, with a small white light beacon.

Skervuile, a larger light beacon in the middle of the sound.

The MacCormaig Isles, off the entrance of Loch Sween.

Carraig an Daimh, an isolated rock 11 metres high 1¾ miles north of MacCormaig Isles.

Ruadh Sgeir at the north end of the sound is 13 metres high with a small light beacon.

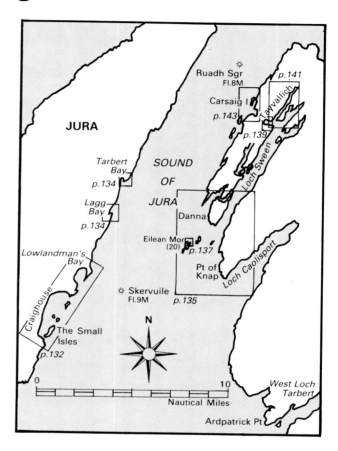

Lights

McArthur's Head lighthouse on the northeast shore of Islay, Fl(2)WR.10s39m14/11M

Na Cuiltean light beacon Fl.10s9m9M

Eilean nan Gabhar (Goat Island) Fl.5s7m8M; at the south entrance to Craighouse Bay, Jura

Nine-foot Rock buoy Q(3)10s; off the entrance to Lowlandman's Bay

Skervuile light beacon Fl.15s22m9M

Ruadh Sgeir light beacon Fl.6s13m8M

Passage notes

There is little to add to the description already given except to emphasise the need to work the tides. If attempting a passage against the tide, some use may be made of eddies in the lee of any projection from the shore, but this will need very careful chartwork, especially on the mainland side. The most useful eddy is off Carsaig Bay.

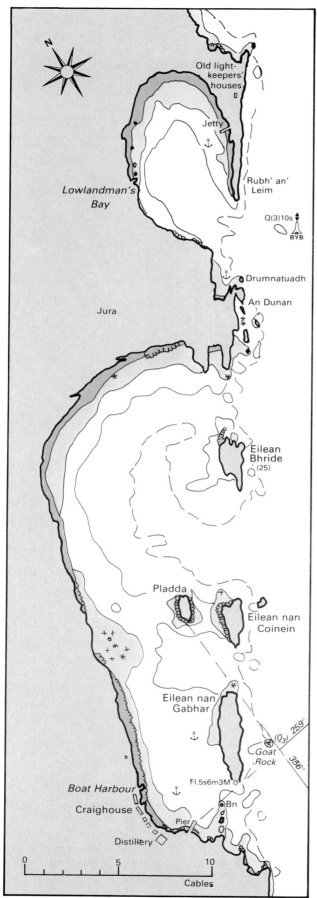

Submerged reefs extend 4 cables NNE of Ruadh Sgeir at the north end of the sound, and there are strong eddies and overfalls north of that islet on the flood. The flood tide sets NNW across the reefs and must be allowed for if passing east of Ruadh Sgeir.

Anchorages on Jura

Craighouse Bay (Loch na Mile)

55°50′N 5°57′W

An extensive bay sheltered by a row of islands, whose south end is 2½ miles from the southeast point of Jura. In spite of the apparent shelter there is often some swell, usually of a tidal origin, and the holding is poor being sand with patches of weed. Visitors' moorings have been laid by the HIDB.

Tides

Tidal streams run strongly across the entrance.

Constant −0130 Oban (+0400 Dover) at springs, and −0430 Oban (+0100 Dover) at neaps.

Height in metres

MHWS	MHWN	MTL	MLWN	MLWS
1·2	0·9	0·7	0·4	0·3

Directions

Na Cuiltean light beacon helps to identify the entrance when approaching from the south, and the distillery and houses are seen once the entrance is opened.

The main entrance is at the south end of the bay, between the south end of Goat Island (Eilean nan Gabhar) and a drying reef extending north from the south point of the bay. A small metal light beacon stands at the south end of Goat Island with the wreck of a puffer below it. An iron beacon with a

Craighouse from southwest. The boat harbour is at bottom left.

ball topmark stands about 20 metres south of the end of the reef (not at the end of the reef) on the south side of the entrance.

Goat Rock 1½ cables east of Goat Island dries 0·3 metres. The end of the concrete pier open of the south end of Goat Island, bearing 259° leads south of the rock, and the islet of Pladda, northwest of Eilean nan Coinein, open of the north end of Goat island 356° leads east of the rock.

At night, Na Cuiltean (Fl.10s9m9M) and the light beacon at the south end of Goat Island (Fl.5s6m3M) make the approach fairly straightforward, but look out for being set off course by the tide which may not be so obvious at night.

Because of the poor holding the HIDB moorings are particularly welcome here. Inshore of the moorings the bay is shoal but there are depths of 2 metres east of the concrete pier, which is usually better sheltered from any swell.

In easterly winds there is slightly better shelter as close to the west side of Goat Island as the depth allows.

At the north end of the bay the bottom is cleaner.

Supplies

Shop, water at pier, diesel, petrol, *Calor Gas*, post office, phone, hotel.

Lowlandman's Bay

55°53′N 5°57′W

The former lighthouse-keepers' houses on the rocky ridge which shelters the east side of the bay are conspicuous, and Ninefoot Rock east cardinal light buoy is east of the entrance.

Much of the bay is shallow and the best anchorage is near the east side, off a stone jetty, southwest of the houses. This bay is also subject to swell with any southerly wind, and there are many shellfish floats around the shore.

Drumnatuadh Bay on the south side of the entrance provides an occasional anchorage in southwesterly winds; the bottom is hard sand.

Further north on Jura several bays provide occasional anchorages but they are all difficult to identify.

Other anchorages

Lagg Bay, 55°56′·5N 5°51′W, 4 miles north of Skervuile was the original landing place for the mail ferry crossing to Jura. Its usefulness as an anchorage is reduced by a power cable which runs down the middle of the bay, but there is space to anchor near the west side. Take care to avoid a submerged rock ½ cable NNE of the east point of the entrance.

Drumnatuadh from northwest.

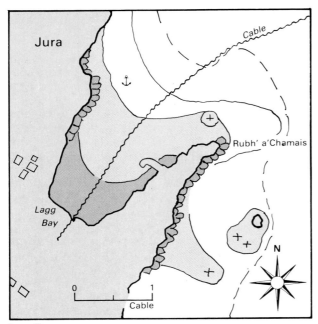

Lagg Bay

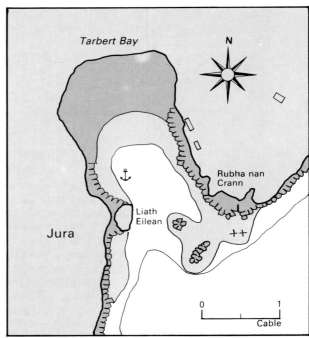

Tarbert Bay

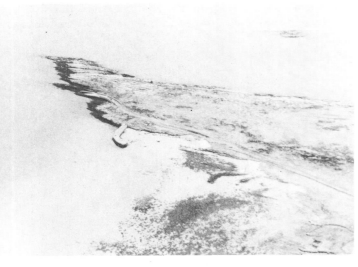

Lagg Bay from west.

Tarbert Bay, 55°58′N 5°50′W, 1½ miles north of Lagg Bay, is identified by a dip in the skyline, as it is only ¾ mile from the head of Loch Tarbert on the west side of Jura. The bay is shallow and almost entirely filled with dense broad-leafed seaweed, but a patch of clear sand north of Liath Eilean has a depth of about 2½ metres (although its extent is said to be diminishing). To avoid the rocks in the entrance pass within ¼ cable of Liath Eilean heading 360°; from north and east pass at least 2 cables south of Rubha nan Crann before turning into the bay.

Lussa Bay, 56°01′N 5°47′W, 3 miles NNE of Tarbert Bay, is straightforward, but give the east point of the entrance a berth of half a cable.

Ardlussa Bay, 56°02′N 5°46′W, 1½ miles NNE of Lussa, provides little shelter except for a shoal-draught boat.

No provisions are available at any of these places.

Anchorages on the east side of the Sound of Jura

MacCormaig Isles and approaches to Loch Sween

55°55′N 5°43′W

Tides (at Craighouse)

Constant −0130 Oban (+0400 Dover) at springs, and −0430 Oban (+0100 Dover) at neaps.

Height in metres

MHWS	MHWN	MTL	MLWN	MLWS
1·2	0·9	0·7	0·4	0·3

Dangers and marks

Most of the dangers in the Sound of Jura are concentrated in this area and affect the approach to Loch Caolisport and Loch Keills (Loch na Cille) as well as Loch Sween. On a direct passage through the sound they are easily avoided by keeping west of Eilean Mor and Carraig an Daimh.

Clearing marks for avoiding these dangers are all fairly distant and not easy to identify, but the plan and illustrations should help. The principal dangers and their clearing marks are as follows, from south to north:

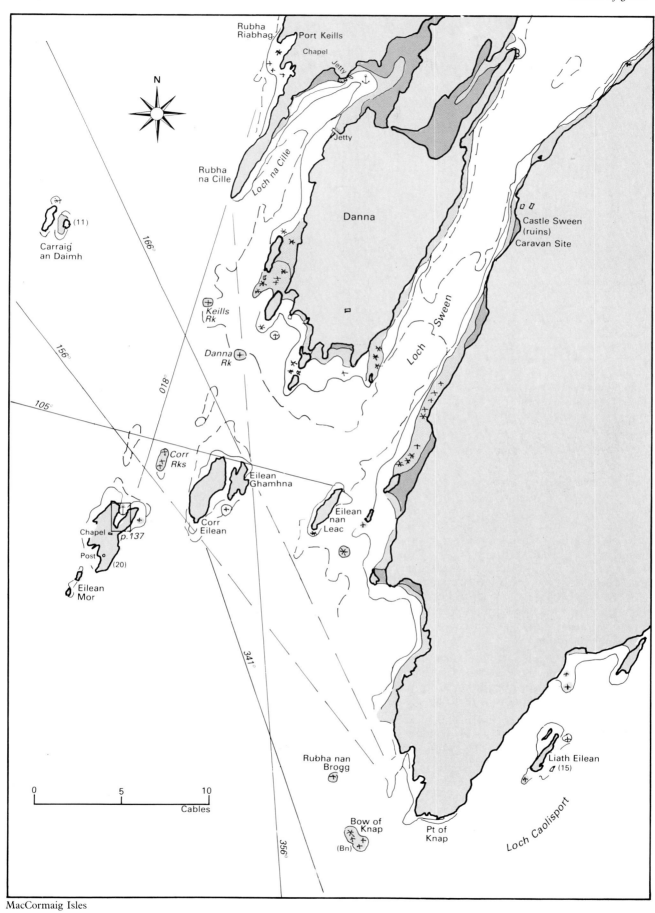

MacCormaig Isles

Bow of Knap; the topmark was missing when the photo was taken.

Danna Rock and Keills Rock both have a least depth of 1·0 metre.

Rubha Riabhag open of Rubha na Cille 018° (see above) leads close west of Keills Rock. The north end of Eilean Ghamhna touching the Point of Knap 154° leads west of these rocks, but take care not to mistake Keppoch Point, 5 miles further south, for the Point of Knap.

Tidal streams

Tides run strongly and irregularly among the Mac-Cormaig Isles and it is essential to watch clearing marks continuously.

The north-going stream begins about +0450 Oban (−0040 Dover) and the south-going stream begins about −0110 Oban (+0545 Dover).

Spring rates off the Point of Knap are 1½ knots. Among the islands and off Rubha na Cille, 2 miles north of the MacCormaig Isles, they are around 3 knots, with eddies and overfalls throughout the area.

Eilean nan Leac   Point of Knap   Corr Eilean

Loch Sween approach – clearing marks for Dana and Keills Rocks from north.

Rubha Riabhaig

Jura   Rubha na Cille   Loch na Cille

Loch Sween approach – clearing marks for Dana and Keills Rocks from south.

Bow of Knap and Ruadh na Brogg, submerged and drying rocks ½ mile west and WSW of the Point of Knap on the north side of the entrance to Loch Caolisport. On the initiative of George Jarvis the CCC has restored a beacon on the Bow of Knap. In 1988 this consisted only of a low concrete drum, but a pole with a triangular topmark is to be replaced on top of the drum.

Rubha na Cille touching Eilean Ghamhna 356° leads 4 cables west of these rocks. Carraig an Daimh touching the southwest point of Corr Eilean 339° leads a cable west of the Bow of Knap.

Corr Rocks, west of the north end of Corr Eilean and NNE of Eilean Mor, nearly uncover, and weed shows at LW neaps.

The Point of Knap just open south of Corr Eilean 143° leads close southwest of Corr Rocks. Rubha Riabhag open west of Rubha na Cille, which looks like a rocky island from this direction, bearing 018° leads a cable west of Corr Rocks. The north end of Eilean nan Leac open north of Eilean Ghamhna 105° leads north of Corr Rocks, but Eilean Puirt Leithe further inshore could be mistaken for Eilean nan Leac, which would take you over the north end of the rocks.

Loch Caolisport

55°53′N 5°40′W

The name is pronounced, and sometimes written as 'Killisport'. There is no shelter for anchoring except in offshore winds, but any submerged hazards within the loch are close inshore, and it is a pleasant place for an occasional visit.

Outside the entrance the Bow of Knap is a dangerous group of drying and submerged rocks 4 cables WSW west of Point of Knap, the north point of the entrance. For marks to clear the west side of these rocks see above. A beacon has been restored on the Bow of Knap, for which see also above. The south side of the Bow of Knap is cleared when Liath Eilean is open south of the Point of Knap.

The best anchorage is near the head of the loch, northeast of Eilean Fada, but there are several inlets, particularly on the northwest side.

Eilean Mor

55°55′N 5°44′W

The most southwesterly of the MacCormaig Isles, identified by the ruined chapel about the middle of the island and a post on a hill top near the south end.

Like other small islands off the west coast, Eilean Mor had a hermit, who lived in a cave near the south end of the island in the 6th century. The chapel was built in the 12th century, and subsequently became a house and was used at one time for illicitly distilling whisky.

Eilean Mor is a popular anchorage, particularly for day visits. The anchorage is a tiny inlet at the north end of the island with an uneven stony bottom and several individual rocks with depths of less than 2 metres.

The ebb tide divides to run past both sides of the island, and particular care needs to be taken to avoid being set off course; a submerged rock lies ½ cable north of the west point of the entrance.

A cairn of stones on the shore at the head of the loch in line with a post on the summit of the island (a concrete replica of an old cross-shaft) leads between two submerged rocks in the basin, but the cairn may be difficult to identify. There is adequate depth of water inshore of both rocks.

The position of the west rock, which has a depth of 0·6 metres, is given by two pairs of painted marks on the west shore in line; the two lines through these marks intersect on the rock. The east rock has a depth of 0·9 metres.

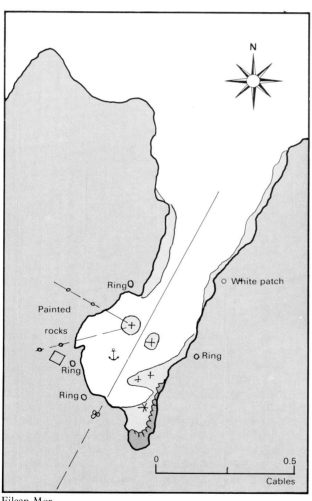

Eilean Mor

Eilean Mor anchorage from east-northeast.

Mooring

The positions of several mooring rings are outlined in white paint; the inlet is very small and the rings may be needed to prevent a yacht swinging, particularly if several others are there. The bottom consists of stones with weed and some sand and the holding is poor in places.

Approach

For dangers and clearing marks in the approach see page 134. Corr Rocks, 3 cables NNE of the entrance are most dangerous if approaching from the north or from Loch Sween.

Eilean Mor anchorage from southwest.

Eilean Mor. The cairn by the shore in line with the post on the hill leads between the submerged rocks.

Loch Sween

55°57′N 5°40′W

A picturesque loch, particularly in its upper parts, with several narrow arms running deep among wooded hills.

Tides

There are no strong tidal streams. There is effectively a 'stand' of tide for three hours at high water from −0330 to −0030 Oban, and +0230 to +0530 Oban at low water. No official figures are available for the rise of tide in Loch Sween; the nearest are for Craighouse: constant −0130 Oban (+0400 Dover) at springs, −0430 Oban (+0100 Dover) at neaps.

Height in metres

MHWS	MHWN	MTL	MLWN	MLWS
1·2	0·9	0·7	0·4	0·3

Dangers and marks

Dangers in the main fairway of the loch are: Lochfoot Rocks (Sgeir Bun an Locha) on the northwest side of the entrance, normally 1 metre above MHWS, but which could be covered during appropriate meteorological conditions; and Sgeirean a'Mhainn, a long rock 0·3 metre high which occasionally covers, about the middle of the loch, 1½ miles NNE of Castle Sween. Just beyond it, Sgeir nan Ron, a cable from the east shore, dries 1·2 metres.

Castle Sween on the east shore is surrounded by a conspicuous caravan park.

Approach

For dangers and clearing marks outside the loch see page 136. To approach by the east side of Eilean nan Leac keep closer to Eilean nan Leac with Castle Sween in sight open of the island 028° to avoid Flat Rock, drying 0·6 metres 2 cables southeast of the island; the passage west of Eilean nan Leac is straightforward.

Approaching from the north part of the Sound of Jura identify the Lochfoot Rocks before turning into the loch. The north end of Corr Eilean in line with the north end of Eilean Mor astern 247° leads southeast of Lochfoot Rocks.

Pass west of the moorings at Castle Sween; there is shoal water inshore both north and south of the moorings.

Identify Sgeirean a'Mhainn and pass it on either side. At high water this rock is not easy to see, and it is best to keep well to the west side of the loch, so as to avoid Sgeir nan Ron also. Beyond this the main fairway of the loch is straightforward.

4½ miles NNE of Castle Sween the loch divides into three parallel branches, with Loch a'Bhealaich (Tayvallich) half a mile to the west.

Anchorage

Taynish Island has an occasional anchorage with limited swinging room north of Taynish Island on the northwest shore of the loch.

Tayvallich

56°01'·5N 5°37'·5W

One of the most perfectly sheltered anchorages on the West Coast, but with several rocks both submerged and above water within. Most of the water deep enough for anchoring is occupied by moorings, but the harbour committee tries to keep two areas clear for visiting yachts to anchor, west and southeast of the central reef. The shores are shoal except on the east side.

Submerged rocks on the north side of the approach are marked by small perches, the first with a triangular topmark, the second T-shaped. If these perches are not seen, keep towards the south shore as Oib Rocks extend halfway across the approach.

Enter by the more southerly of the two gaps in the outer reef as the other is foul; turn to port and anchor clear of the central reef. This anchorage is deep, and the alternative is to pass round either end of the central reef and anchor to the west of it.

A submerged rock off the south end of the central reef is marked by a small south cardinal buoy which must be passed on its south side. If the buoy cannot be seen, a clearing mark is the south gable of the post office just open; the post office is a buff-coloured building with a red roof by the shore.

In the passage north of the central reef a small starboard-hand beacon marks a submerged rock on the north side of the passage. The wooden pier at the northwest side of the bay is used by fishing boats; all vessels are requested not to lie alongside for more than an hour.

An alternative anchorage is outside the bay to the south of the entrance, but the bottom consists of boulders and the holding may not be good in strong winds.

Supplies

Grocer at post office towards the south end of the village. Water tap at the shop, with a pipe to a buoy directly off the post office for filling a boat's tanks (ask to use when buying stores). Phone box beside post office. Refuse disposal skip beside post office. *Calor Gas* at caravan site at north side of the bay. Restaurant. No fuel.

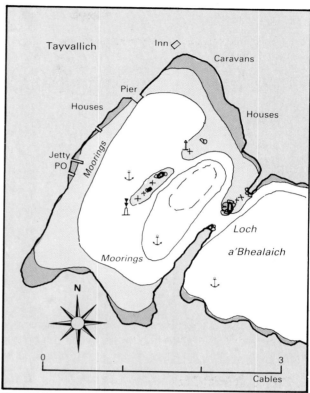

Tayvallich

Caol Scotnish

56°02'N 5°36'W

A narrow inlet two miles long and in places only ¼ cable wide with sheer rocky sides; the upper parts are used for fish farming.

Oib Rocks, a cable south of the entrance, are marked by a perch with a triangular topmark, but there is a submerged rock about 30 metres SSW of the perch; rocks west of the entrance are marked by a perch with a T-shaped topmark. If the Oib Rocks perch is missing keep closer to the south shore until Caol Scotnish is well open.

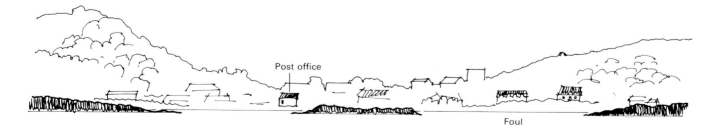

Tayvallich approach.

Tayvallich from southeast.

Tayvallich and Caol Scotnish from south.

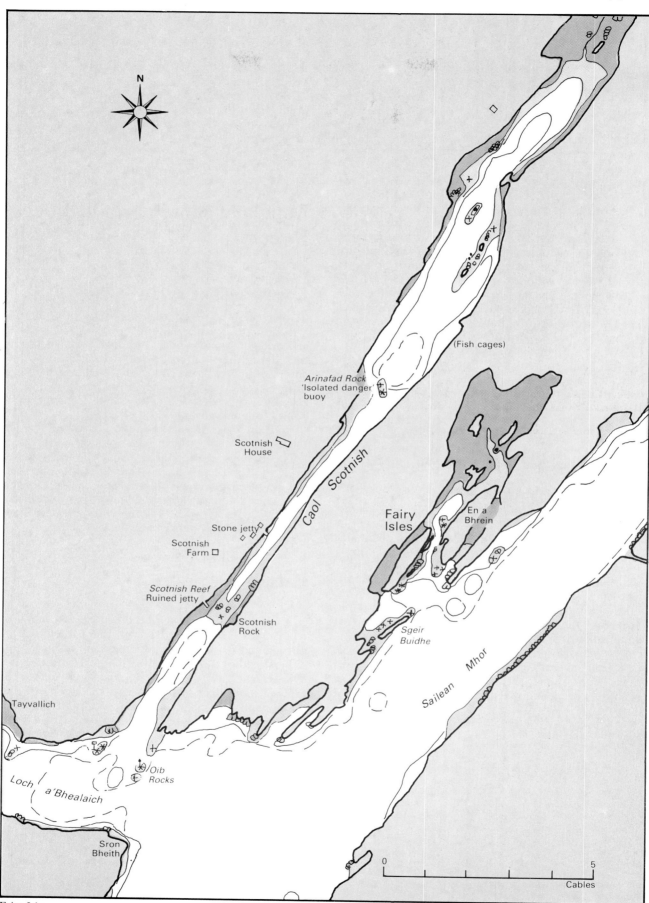

(Fish cages)

Arinafad Rock
'Isolated danger'
buoy

Scotnish
House

Caol Scotnish

**Fairy
Isles**

En a
Bhrein

Stone jetty

Scotnish
Farm

Scotnish Reef
Ruined jetty

Scotnish
Rock

*Sgeir
Buidhe*

Sailean   Mhor

Tayvallich

Oib
Rocks

Loch   a'Bhealaich

Sron
Bheith

0   5

Cables

Fairy Isles

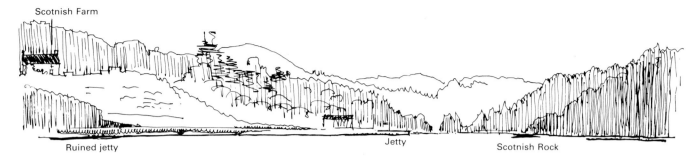

Scotnish Farm

Ruined jetty   Jetty   Scotnish Rock

Caol Scotnish approach.

The main hazards are Scotnish Reef and Scotnish Rocks, 3 cables from the entrance and a cable south of the narrowest part. Scotnish Rocks rarely cover and should be passed close on their west side to avoid the reef; the passage between them is no more than 20 metres wide.

Half a mile beyond a stone pier on the west side of the narrows, where the kyle opens up, Arinafad Rock which dries just west of mid-channel is usually marked by a small buoy with a topmark of two balls, but it might be confused with other buoys at the fish farm, particularly if its topmark is missing.

In the rest of the inlet most rocks are above water, but there are some drying rocks off the west shore south of a caravan which is SSW of a wooded bank. The head of Caol Scotnish dries 2 cables but the basin before the head is clean. Mud in mid-channel is very soft and if anchoring ensure that the anchor is well dug in.

Fairy Isles

56°02′N 5°35′·5W

An inlet on the west side of Sailein Mhor, the main arm of the head of the loch. The most straightforward anchorage is northwest of Sgeir Buidhe at the south end of the inlet. Keep 50 metres off the north end of Sgeir Buidhe to avoid a 1-metre rock. The north part of the inlet is full of rocks and some years ago the remains of the submerged barrier of an abandoned fish farm was reported to be a hazard.

The most easterly arm at the head of Loch Sween is un-named and much of it is occupied by fish cages. Port Lunna, the inlet north of Eilean Loain, is entirely occupied by fish cages.

Mainland shore north of Loch Sween

Loch Keills (Loch na Cille)

2 miles north of the MacCormaig Isles, Loch Keills is clean with a sandy bottom but the head is shoal and dries for about a mile. Although it is exposed to the south, the strong tidal streams across the entrance tend to keep any swell out of the loch except, of course, at slack water. Anchor just short of a jetty on the northwest side, 1 mile from the west point of the entrance.

Note the clearing marks for Keills Rock on page 136.

The passage inside Eilean nan Coinean, 4 miles ENE of Rubha na Cille, is littered with rocks but can be puzzled out in quiet weather with a large-scale chart; no clearing marks have been identified. The passage between Eilean Dubh and Eilean Traighe has a least depth of about 0·7 metres.

Carsaig

56°02′N 5°39′W

It is quite easy to mistake the bay north of Eilean nan Coinean for Carsaig Bay, but there are houses at Carsaig and the gap in the skyline there is lower.

Tidal eddies run across the mouth of Carsaig Bay. The entrance to it is partly blocked by a reef which extends more than halfway across the bay from the north point in a SSW direction. Rocks in the bay, both submerged and drying, lie up to 2 cables from the shore, and the parts of the bay which are clear of rocks are full of weed. A power cable crossing to Jura runs out in a northerly direction from a beacon on the south shore.

There is some shelter in either of two inlets southwest of Carsaig Bay, between Eilean Dubh and Eilean Traighe, and between Eilean Traighe and the mainland. Rows of buoys across the mouth of these bays are said to be mooring pickups for fishing boats, not fish-farming equipment; there is space to anchor clear of them, but most of the inlet east of Eilean Traighe dries.

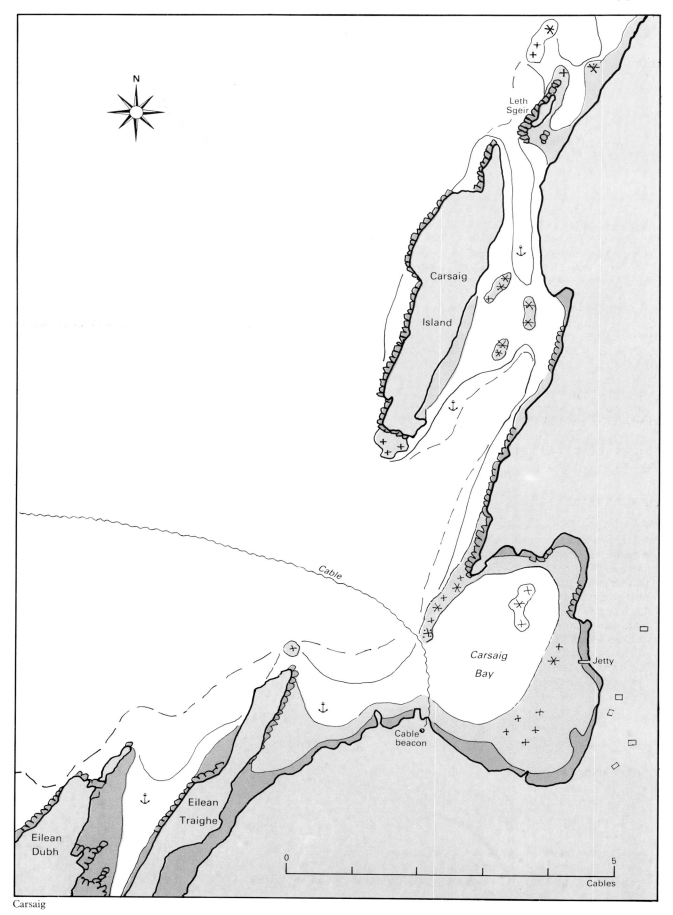

Leth
Sgeir

Carsaig

Island

Cable

Carsaig
Bay

Jetty

Cable
beacon

Eilean
Traighe

Eilean
Dubh

0   5

Cables

Carsaig

Carsaig from southwest.

The sound between Carsaig Island and the mainland provides some shelter close to the island, but
there are yacht moorings, and drying rocks to be
avoided.

Except in northerly winds, the best shelter is east
of the north part of Carsaig Island. Approach from
northwest keeping closer to Carsaig Island than to
Leth Sgeir which has drying reefs off its southwest
end. A narrow passage 3 metres deep runs within 20
metres of the promontory on the mainland side
northeast of the drying rocks but the tide runs fast
here at times and the passage should be investigated
first with a dinghy.

Supplies

At Tayvallich (*see page 139*) ½ mile by road from
the jetty in Carsaig Bay.

Other anchorages

Sailean Mor, 2 miles NNE of Carsaig Bay, provides
an occasional anchorage but it is exposed to any
sea from the north, and the head of the bay dries
for 2 cables.

Loch Crinan has a straightforward anchorage off the
hotel on the south shore of the loch, uncomfortable in strong west or northwest winds. Complete
shelter may be found in the canal basin.

Appendix

I. CHARTS AND OTHER PUBLICATIONS

The Imray charts *C63* and *C64* at a scale of 1:150,000 cover all the places in this volume. They are available at most chandlers and from the Clyde Cruising Club, usually folded, but for any boat which has a large enough chart table it is better to order a flat copy, or one laminated in plastic.

A general chart for the whole west coast of Scotland is Admiralty chart *2635* at a scale of 1:500,000.

The following Admiralty charts relate to the waters covered by this volume. Some of these are essential, and the more you have, the less your pilotage will be fraught with anxiety. The relevant Ordnance Survey maps are also listed.

Chart	Title	Scale
2635	West Coast of Scotland	500,000
2724	North Channel to Firth of Lorne	200,000
OS76	Girvan	50,000
OS82	Stranraer & Glen Luce	50,000

Chart	Title – areas in Chapter I	Scale
2198	North Channel, South Part	75,000
2199	North Channel, North Part	75,000
2126	Approaches to Firth of Clyde	75,000
1403	Loch Ryan	10,000
1866	Plan of Girvan	6,250
OS69	Island of Arran	50,000
OS70	Ayr & Kilmarnock	50,000

Chart	Title – areas in Chapter II	Scale
2126	Approaches to Firth of Clyde	75,000
2131	Firth of Clyde and Loch Fyne	75,000
2798	Lough Foyle to Sanda	75,000
2220	Pladda to Ardrossan	36,000
2221	Ardrossan to Kilbrannan Sound	36,000
1866	Plans of Ayr, Troon, Irvine, Ardrossan	6,250 to 10,000
1864	Plan of Lamlash Harbour	20,000
1866	Plans of Millport and Largs Channel	12,500
1907	Little Cumbrae to Cloch Point	25,000
OS69	Island of Arran	50,000
OS70	Ayr & Kilmarnock	50,000

Chart	Title – areas in Chapter III	Scale
2131	Firth of Clyde and Loch Fyne	75,000
1994	Approaches to River Clyde	15,000
3746	Loch Long and Loch Goil	25,000
3740	Upper Loch Long	10,000
2000	Gareloch and Approaches	10,000
2007	River Clyde	15,000
OS56	Loch Lomond	50,000
OS63	Firth of Clyde	50,000
OS64	Glasgow	50,000

Chart	Title – areas in Chapter IV	Scale
2131	Firth of Clyde and Loch Fyne	75,000
1906	Kyles of Bute	25,000
2381	Loch Fyne, Lower Part	25,000
2382	Loch Fyne, Upper Part	25,000
OS55	Lochgilphead	50,000
OS56	Loch Lomond	50,000

OS62	North Kintyre	50,000
OS63	Firth of Clyde	50,000

Chart	Title – areas in Chapter V	Scale
2798	Lough Foyle to Sanda	75,000
2126	Approaches to Firth of Clyde	75,000
2168	Approaches to Sound of Jura	75,000
2383	Inchmarnock Water	25,000
2475	Sound of Gigha	25,000
2477	West Loch Tarbert	25,000
OS62	North Kintyre	50,000
OS68	South Kintyre	50,000
OS69	Island of Arran	50,000

Chart	Title – areas in Chapter VI	Scale
2168	Approaches to Sound of Jura	75,000
2474	Plan of Port Ellen	15,000
OS60	Islay	50,000

Chart	Title – areas in Chapter VII	Scale
2168	Approaches to Sound of Jura	75,000
2169	Approaches to Firth of Lorne	75,000
2481	Sound of Islay	25,000
2474	Scalasaig and Loch Staosnaig	12,500
OS61	Jura & Colonsay	50,000

Chart	Title – areas in Chapter VII	Scale
2168	Approaches to Sound of Jura	75,000
2169	Approaches to Firth of Lorne	75,000
2396	Sound of Jura, South Part	25,000
2397	Sound of Jura, North Part	25,000
OS55	Lochgilphead	50,000
OS61	Jura & Colonsay	50,000
OS62	North Kintyre	50,000

Order charts early so that you have time to order more, if it looks as though your first choice is not enough. There are Admiralty chart agents throughout Britain, and in most other countries. Chart agents on the West Coast are:

Kelvin Hughes, Glasgow ☎ 041-221 5452
Christie and Wilson, Glasgow ☎ 041-552 7137
W. B. Leitch and Son, Tarbert ☎ (088 02) 287
Crinan Boats, Crinan ☎ (054 683) 232

Don't rely on buying charts locally without ordering in advance – they may not be in stock. Some other chandlers stock Admiralty charts, although sometimes at a higher cost.

Imray, Laurie, Norie & Wilson Ltd are Admiralty chart agents and will supply charts by post; Wych House, The Broadway, St Ives, Huntingdon, Cambridgeshire PE17 4BT, ☎ (0480) 62114, telex 329195 Imrays G, fax (0480) 496109.

Some charts which have long been discontinued provide much more detail, at a larger scale, than any now published for the same area. Most relevant here is *2418* of Colonsay and Oronsay at 1:24,430. All older charts, particularly the fine Victorian engravings, show more detail inshore and on land than the current publications, although they may be less accurate. Old charts should only be used to supplement current ones, not as a substitute for them.

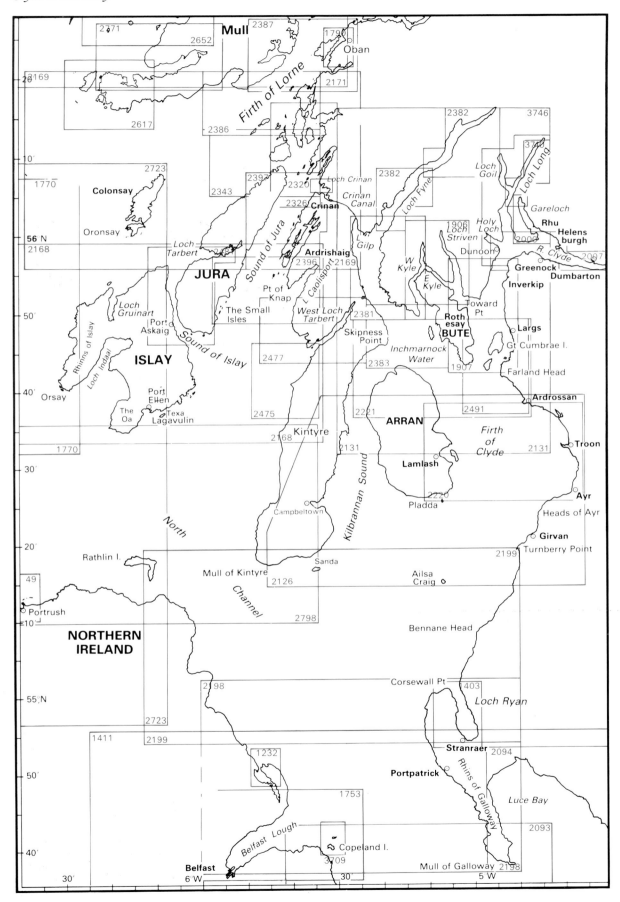

Photocopies of old charts – of editions not less than 50 years old, for copyright reasons – may be obtained from the National Library of Scotland Map Room Annexe, 137 Causewayside, Edinburgh 9, ☎ (031) 667 7848. They can provide either a single photographic copy of the whole sheet, or more quickly a patchwork of A3-size pages.

Current charts show much less detail ashore than older charts, and Ordnance Survey maps at a scale of 1:50,000, or Bartholomew maps at 1:100,000 help to fill in the picture.

A set of 50 sketch charts published by the Clyde Cruising Club is available from chandlers or direct from the CCC at SV Carrick, Clyde Street, Glasgow G1 4LN. These charts are convenient to use because of their size, but the relevant Admiralty charts should also be carried.

The Clyde Cruising Club *Sailing Directions and Anchorages* are also available from the CCC at the above address.

The Admiralty *West Coast of Scotland Pilot* (NP 66), with supplements up to date, is a most valuable publication.

The Admiralty tidal stream atlas for the *North Coast of Ireland and West Coast of Scotland* (NP 218) is very useful.

Tide tables are essential, preferably for Greenock and Oban and giving heights of each high and low water; often supplied by local chandlers, boatyards and marinas, as well as chandlers in Glasgow. A new almanac published annually from 1989 is the *Malin, Hebrides and Minches Edition* of the *Yachtsman's Almanac*, available from chandlers or post-free from the publishers, Clyde Marine Press, Westgate, Toward, Argyll PA23 7UA, at £7·50. There are of course the full *Admiralty Tide Tables* Vol. 1 (NP 201) or Brown's, Macmillan's or Reed's Almanac.

Pilotage books

Scottish West Coast Pilot, Mark Brackenbury, Stanford 1981

Clyde Cruising Club Sailing Directions: Kintyre to Ardnamurchan, 1981

Clyde Cruising Club Sailing Directions: Firth of Clyde, 1988

West Coast of Scotland Pilot, Hydrographer of the Navy, 1974

General books

Scottish Lighthouses, R. W. Munro, Thule Press, 1979

The Islands of Western Scotland, W. H. Murray, Eyre Methuen, 1973

Companion Guide to the Western Highlands of Scotland, W. H. Murray, Collins

Exploring Scotland's Heritage – Argyll and the Western Isles Graham Ritchie and Mary Harman, HMSO 1985

The Clyde Estuary and Central Region J. B. Stevenson, HMSO 1985

The Islands of Scotland, Norman Tennent, Scottish Mountaineering Trust, 1976 (for climbers and hillwalkers)

Para Handy Tales, Neil Munro, Pan Books, 1981 (short stories of the crew of a Clyde Puffer from the beginning of the century)

The Islands of the Clyde, R. A. Downie, Melvin Press, 1982 Kintyre, David and Charles

Kintyre, Alasdair Carmichael, David and Charles

Clyde Navigation, J. F. Riddell, John Donald, 1979 (a fairly specialised history of the development of the Clyde)

Islay, biography of an island, M. C. Storrie, Oa Press, 1981

II. GLOSSARY OF GAELIC WORDS WHICH COMMONLY APPEAR IN PLACE NAMES

Many varieties of spelling are found, so it is as well to search for possible alternatives; variations of the same word are listed together but usually at least have the same initial letter. Many words beginning with a consonant take an 'h' after the initial letter in certain cases; notably in adjectives the genitive and the feminine gender and genitive cases of nouns, so that most of the words below could have an 'h' as the second letter.

There is no possibility of guiding the reader on pronunciation except to say that consonants followed by an 'h' are not often pronounced, and that 'mh' and 'bh' at the beginning of a word are pronounced as (and of course in anglicised versions often spelt with) a 'v'. *Mhor* is pronounced – approximately – *vore*; *claidheamh* is something like *clayeh*, and *bogha* is *bo'a*.

Some names, particularly those of islands ending in 'a' or 'ay', are of Norse origin. Anyone at all familiar with French and Latin will see correspondences there, for example Caisteil – also Eaglais and Teampuill.

Many words are compounds made up of several often quite common parts, frequently linked by *na/nam/nan*. The following are the most usual forms of words which commonly occur in Gaelic place names. They often set out to describe the physical features and so give some clues to identification. Some of them occur almost everywhere; most lochs have a Sgeir More and an Eilean Dubh, or vice versa.

Gaelic	*English*
a, am, an, an t-	the
abhainn (avon)	river
acairseid	harbour (acair = anchor)
achadh (ach, auch)	field
allt	stream, burn
ard, aird	promontory
aros	house
ba	cattle
bairneach	limpet
bagh ('bay')	bay
ban	white, pale; female (ban-righ = queen), as noun: woman
bealach	narrow passage
beg, beag, beaga	small
ben, beinn	mountain
beul (bel)	mouth of (belnahua = mouth of the cave)
bodach	old man
bogha (bo')	a detached rock, usually one which uncovers
breac	speckled (as noun: trout)
buachaille	shepherd
buidhe (bhuidhe, buie)	yellow (also: pleasing)
bun	mouth of a river
cailleach	old woman
caisteil	castle
camas	bay
caol (a' chaolais)	narrow passage (kyle)
caorach	sheep
ceall, cille (kil...)	monastic cell, church
ceann (kin...)	head
clachan	usually a group of houses (clach = stone)
claidheamh	sword (hence 'claymore' = great sword)
cnoc (knock)	rounded hill
coire (corrie)	cauldron, hollow among hills, whirlpool
craobh	tree
creag	cliff, rock (crag)
darroch	oak tree
dearg ('jerrig')	red
deas	south
dobhran	otter
donn	brown (dun)
druim	ridge
dubh (dhu)	black, dark, (disastrous)
dun, duin	fortified place, usually prehistoric
each	horse
ear	east
eilean (or eileach)	island
fada	long
fir, fear	man
fraoch, fraoich	heather
garbh	rough
geal	white
gille	boy
glas	grey (sometimes green)
gobhar (gour)	goat (gabhar = she-goat)
gorm	blue
gamhna	stirk, year-old calf
iar	west (easily confused with Ear)
iolair	eagle
keills, kells	church
kin... (ceann)	head of
liath	grey
mara	sea
meadhonach	middle-sized
meall	lump, knob
mor (more, mhor, vore)	large, great (often only relative)
muc, muck	pig (often a sea-pig = porpoise or a whale)
na, na h-, nam, nan	of (the)
naomh (nave, neave)	holy, saint
...nish (ness)	point of land
poll, puill	pool
righ ('ree')	king
ron, roin	seal
ruadh	red, reddish
rudha (rhu)	point of land, promontory
sailean	creek
sgeir, sgeirean (skerry)	rock, above water or covering
sron	nose (as a headland)
sruth	stream, current
tigh	house
tober	well
traigh	beach
tuath (or tuadh)	north
uamh	cave

III. QUICK REFERENCE TABLE OF PROVISIONS, SERVICES AND SUPPLIES

Place, grouped in sequence of chapters	Diesel	Petrol	Calor Gas	Water hose	Water, nearby	Chandlery	Charts	Boatyard	Moorings (vis)	Moorings (l/t)	Pontoon berths	Launching place	Provisions	Hotel	Restaurant	Showers	Laundrette	Bank	Refuse disposal
Portpatrick	●	●	●		●						●		●	●	●			●	●
Stranraer	●	●	●	●							●		●	●	●			●	●
Ballantrae					●						●		●	●					
Girvan	●	●	●	●		●		●					●	●			●	●	●
Maidens	●	●	●		●							●	●	●	●			●	●
Dunure		●			●								●	●	●				
Ayr	●	●	●	●		●		●	●		●		●	●	●			●	●
Troon	●	●	●	●		●		●			●		●	●	●	●	●	●	●
Irvine					●						●		●	●					
Saltcoats													●	●					
Ardrossan				●									●	●					
Lamlash	●	●			●	●							●	●					
Brodick	●	●	●		●								●	●					
Millport	●	●	●		●								●	●					
Largs	●	●	●			●		●			●	●	●	●		●			●
Wemyss Bay	●	●			●								●	●	●	●			●
Inverkip	●	●	●			●		●			●	●	●	●	●	●	●		●
Dunoon	●	●											●	●					
Holy Loch	●	●											●	●					
Lochgoilhead	●	●	●		●					●			●	●	●				
Arrochar	●	●	●										●	●	●				
Helensburgh	●	●											●	●					
Rhu Marina	●	●	●	●		●		●			●	●	●	●				●	●
Garelochead	●	●											●	●				●	
Gourock	●	●						●					●	●					
Dumbarton	●	●			●	●		●			●	●	●	●				●	
Renfrew	●	●			●	●		●			●	●	●	●				●	
Rothesay	●	●	●		●	●					●		●	●	●			●	
Port Bannatyne	●	●	●		●			●					●	●				●	
Colintraive					●								●	●					
Tighnabruaich	●	●	●		●			●					●	●					
Tarbert	●	●	●	●		●	●	●			●	●	●	●	●	●	●	●	●
Ardrishaig	●	●	●	●				●			●	●	●	●	●	●		●	●
Lochgilphead	●	●											●	●				●	
Loch Gair													●						
Inveraray	●	●	●										●	●				●	
Loch Ranza			●		●							●	●	●	●				
Carradale			●			●			●		●		●	●	●				
Campbeltown	●	●	●		●			●	●		●	●	●	●	●	●		●	
Ardminish	●	●	●		●					●			●	●	●			●	
Portnahaven							●						●	●					
Port Ellen	●	●			●								●	●				●	
Port Askaig	●	●	●	●							●		●	●					
Scalasaig		●									●		●	●					
Craighouse	●	●	●		●						●		●	●					
Tayvallich			●	●									●	●	●				

Notes

Diesel may not be available by the water and may have to be carried some distance. Petrol will usually have to be carried. Reference to pontoon berths includes berths alongside a quay.

IV· CONVERSION TABLES

metres–feet

m	ft/m	ft
0·3	1	3·3
0·6	2	6·6
0·9	3	9·8
1·2	4	13·1
1·5	5	16·4
1·8	6	19·7
2·1	7	23·0
2·4	8	26·2
2·7	9	29·5
3·0	10	32·8
6·1	20	65·6
9·1	30	98·4
12·2	40	131·2
15·2	50	164·0
30·5	100	328·1

centimetres–inches

cm	in/cm	in
2·5	1	0·4
5·1	2	0·8
7·6	3	1·2
10·2	4	1·6
12·7	5	2·0
15·2	6	2·4
17·8	7	2·8
20·3	8	3·1
22·9	9	3·5
25·4	10	3·9
50·8	20	7·9
76·2	30	11·8
101·6	40	15·7
127·0	50	19·7
254·0	100	39·4

metres–fathoms–feet

m	fathoms	ft
0·9	0·5	3
1·8	1	6
3·7	2	12
5·5	3	18
7·3	4	24
9·1	5	30
11·0	6	36
12·8	7	42
14·6	8	48
16·5	9	54
18·3	10	60
36·6	20	120
54·9	30	180
73·2	40	240
91·4	50	300

kilometres–statute miles

km	M/km	M
1·6	1	0·6
3·2	2	1·2
4·8	3	1·9
6·4	4	2·5
8·0	5	3·1
9·7	6	3·7
11·3	7	4·3
12·9	8	5·0
14·5	9	5·6
16·1	10	6·2
32·2	20	12·4
48·3	30	18·6
64·4	40	24·9
80·5	50	31·1
120·7	75	46·6
160·9	100	62·1
402·3	250	155·3
804·7	500	310·7
1609·3	1000	621·4

kilograms–pounds

kg	lb/kg	lb
0·5	1	2·2
0·9	2	4·4
1·4	3	6·6
1·8	4	8·8
2·3	5	11·0
2·7	6	13·2
3·2	7	15·4
3·6	8	17·6
4·1	9	19·8
4·5	10	22·0
9·1	20	44·1
13·6	30	66·1
18·1	40	88·2
22·7	50	110·2
34·0	75	165·3
45·4	100	220·5
113·4	250	551·2
226·8	500	1102·3
453·6	1000	2204·6

litres–gallons

l	gal/l	gal
4·5	1	0·2
9·1	2	0·4
13·6	3	0·7
18·2	4	0·9
22·7	5	1·1
27·3	6	1·3
31·8	7	1·5
36·4	8	1·8
40·9	9	2·0
45·5	10	2·2
90·9	20	4·4
136·4	30	6·6
181·8	40	8·8
227·3	50	11·0
341·0	75	16·5
454·6	100	22·0
1136·5	250	55·0
2273·0	500	110·0
4546·1	1000	220·0

Index

aerobeacons, 3
Ailsa Craig, 18
Am Far Eilean, 120, 122
An Sailein, 124
anchorages, 3-5
anchors, 2
Ardentinny, 46
Ardgartan Point, 49
Ardlamont Bay, 68
Ardlussa Bay, 134
Ardmaleish Boat Building Co., 59
Ardmarnock Bay, 68
Ardminish, 96-98
Ardmore Channel, 44
Ardmore Islands, inshore passage, 113-117
Ardnadam, 45
Ardrishaig, 73, 74
Ardrossan, 29-30
Aros Bay, 116, 117
Arran
east coast, 30-34
north coast, 84-85, 87
Arrochar, 49
Asgog Bay, 68
Association of Scottish Yacht Charterers, 2
Auchgoyle Bay, 80
Ayr, 22-23
Heads of, 15-20

Bagh Buic (Buck Bay), 68
Bagh Gleann Righ Beag, 124
Bagh Gleann Righ Mor, 124
Ballantrae, 16
Ballochmartin Bay, 39
Balnakailly Bay, 62
Barmore Island, 72
Barrfields Slip, 39
Black Farland Bay, 65
Black Harbour, 68
Blackwaterfoot, 87
Blairmore, 46
Blindman's Bay, 65
Bowling Basin, 54, 56
Bowmore, 107, 108
Brodick, 33-34
Bruichladdich, 107
Buck Bay, 68
Buck Sound, 68
Bunnahaven, 122
Burnt Islands, 60-62

Cairndow, 81
Cairnryan, 13
Caladh Harbour, 63-64
Campbeltown Harbour, 89-90
Campbeltown Lock, 87-89
Campbeltown Shipyard, 90

Caol Ila Distillery, 122
Caol Scotnish, 139, 140-142
Caolas an Eilean, 110
Caolas Gigalum, 96
Caolas Mor, Oronsay, 129
Caolas Port na Lice, 113-115
Cara, 93, 94
Carradale Bay, 86-87
Carradale Harbour (Port Crannaich), 86
Carrick Castle, 47-48
Carsaig, 142-144
Carskey Bay, 92
chartering and instruction, 2
charts, 1, 7
Clyde, Firth of *see* Firth of Clyde
Clyde, River, 53-56
Clyde Coastguard, 7
Clyde Cruising Club, 1, 4, 8
Clyde Marine Press, 8
Clyde River Boat Yard, Renfrew, 55
Clynder, 52
coast radio stations, 6
coastguards, 6, 7
Colintraive, 62
Colonsay and Oronsay, 119, 127-130
communications, 6-7
conversion tables, 150
Cove Bay, 46
Craighouse Bay, 132-133
Crarae Bay, 80
Crinan Canal, 75-77
Culzean Bay, 18
Cumbrae Isles, 35-37
Cumhann Beag, 125-127

Davaar, Island, 87, 88
Deuchlands, the (Dubh-chaol Linne), 72
diesel, 149
Druimyeon Bay, 98
Dubh-chaol Linne, 72
Dumbarton, 55-56
Dunoon, 39
Dunure, 20

East Kyle, 60-62
approaches, 57-60
East Tarbert Bay, Gigha, 98
East Tarbert Bay, Mull of Galloway, 9
Eilean Buidhe, 68
Eilean Craobhach, 113-115
Eilean Dearg, 64
Eilean Garbh, Gigha, 98
Eilean Mor (MacCormaig Isles), 137

Eilean Traighe, 101
emergencies, 7
equipment, 2
Erskine Bridge, 54
Ettrick Bay, 65

FHG Publications, 2
Fairy Isles, 142
Faslane, 52
ferries, 2
Finart Bay, Ardentinny, 46
Finnart Oil Terminal, 46, 49
Finnarts Bay, 15
Firth of Clyde, 21-41
approaches, 9-20
channel, 34-35, 44
head of, 43-53
fishing and fish farms, 4
Furnace, 80

Galloway, Mull of, 9
Galloway, Rhins of, 9-11
Gareloch, 49-52
Garelochhead, 52
Getting around the Highlands and Islands, 2
Gibb's Point, 45
Gigalum, 93, 94
Caolas, 96
Gigha, Sound of, 92-96
Gigha Engineering, 98
Girvan, 16-18
Girvan Chandlers, 18
Glac Mhor and Glac Bheag, 73
Glas Uig, 116, 117
Glenan Bay, 68
Glenbatrick Bay, 124
Glencallum Bay, 35
Glenmallan Jetty, 46, 49
Goodwin, J., Ayr, 23
Gourock Bay, 53
Great Cumbrae, 36-37
Grogport, 85
Gunna Sound, 130

harbours, 5
Heads of Ayr, 15-20
Helensburgh, 53
Highlands and Islands Development Board (HIDB), 2, 5
Holy Island, Lamlash Bay, 32, 33
Holy Loch, 44-45
Hunter's Quay, 45
Hunterston Channel, 34, 35

Inchmarnock, 65-67
Innellan, 39
Inveraray, 81

Irvine, 26-28
Island Davaar, 87, 88
Islay
northwest coast, 122
Sound of, 119-127
south coast, 103-117

jetties, 5
Jura
Loch Tarbert, 123-127
other anchorages, 132-134
Sound of, 131-144

Kames, West Kyle, 65
Kames Bay (Port Bannatyne), 58-59
Kennacraig, 99
Kilbrannan Sound, 84
Kilbride Bay, 68
Kilchattan Bay, 35
Kilcreggan, 49
Channel, 44
Kildalloig Bay, 88
Kildalton Bay (Loch a'Chnuic), 115
Kildonald Bay, 87
'Killisport', 136
Kilmun, 45
Kintyre, 83-101
Mull of, 90-92
Kip Marina, 40-41
Kyles of Bute, 57-67
East Kyle, 60-62
approaches, 57-60
West Kyle, 65-67
Kyles of Bute Sailing Club, 58

Lady Bay, 15
Lagavulin Bay, 111-113
Lagg Bay, 133, 134
Lamlash Bay, 9, 21, 32-33
Largs, 2
Channel, 38-39
Pier, 53
Yacht Haven, 21, 38-39
launching, 2
Leitch, W. B., Tarbert, 72
lifeboats, 7
lights, 3
Little Cumbrae, 35
Loch Caolisport ('Killisport'), 136
Loch a'Chnuic (Kildalton Bay), 115
Loch na Cille (Loch Keills), 142
Loch Crinan, 144
Loch Fyne
Lower, 66-74
Upper, 78-81

Loch Gair, 79
Loch Gilp, 72-73
Loch Goil, 47-49
Loch Goil Cruisers, 49
Loch Gruinart, 122
Loch Indaal, 107
Loch Keills (Loch na Cille), 142
Loch Long, 46, 49-53
    Channel, 44
Loch na Mile (Craighouse Bay), 132-133
Loch Ranza, 84-85
Loch Riddon, 64-65
Loch Ryan, 9, 13-14
    to Heads of Ayr, 15-20
Loch Staosnaig, 129
Loch Stornoway, 101
Loch Striven, 59
Loch Sween, 138-142
    approaches to, 134-136
Loch an t-Sailean, 111-113
Loch Tarbert, Jura, 123-127
Loch Tarbert, West, 99-101
Lochgoilhead, 48, 49
Lowlandman's Bay, 133
Lussa Bay, 134

McAlister's Yard, Dumbarton, 55
MacCallum, A., Tarbert, 72
MacCormaig Isles, 134-138
McGruer's Yacht Yard, Rosneath Bay, 52
Machrihanish Bay, 92
Macintyre, Peter (Clyde) Ltd., 59
Mackay, J. W., Ayr, 23
Maidens Harbour, 18
Malin, Hebrides and Minches Edition (Yachtsman's Almanac), 8
maps, 2
marinas, 5
marine rescue sub-centre, 7
Marine Services Scotland, Renfrew, 55
Millport, 36-37
Minard Bay, 80
Minard Narrows, 80
Modern Charters, Clynder, 52
moorings, 3-5
Mull of Galloway, 9
Mull of Kintyre, 90-92

Nave Island, 122, 123
Newtown, 80, 81
Newtown Bay, 81
Nicholson Hughes Sailmakers, 52
Nobles, Alex, and Sons, Ltd., Givern, 18

On the water, 2
One Tree Island, 64
Ormidale, 64
Oronsay and Colonsay, 119, 127-130
Otter Ferry, 79
Otter Spit, 78

passage making, 2
piers, 5
pilotage directions notes on, 7-8
place names, 6-7
Pladda, 31
plans, notes on, 7-8
Plod Sgeirean, 115
Port Ann, 78
Port Askaig, 120, 121
Port Bannatyne, 58-59
Port Charlotte, 107
Port Crannaich, 86
Port Ellen, 107-110
Port Mor, Gigha, 98
Port Mor, Islay, 116, 117
Portavadie, 68
Portnahaven, 105, 106, 107
Portpatrick, 11-12
provisions, 149
public transport, 2

radiobeacons, 3
radiotelephones, 6
Renfrew Harbour, 55, 56
Rhins of Galloway, 9-11
Rhu Bay, 52
Rhu Marina, 51-52
Rhu Narrows, 49-52
Rosneath Bay, 52
Rothesay Bay, 58
Rothesay Sound, 57-59
Royal Highland Yacht Club, 13

Saddell Bay, 87
Sailean Mor, 144
sailmaker, 52, 53, 72
St Catherine's, 81
St Ninian's Bay, 65
Saltcoats, 28
Salthouse, 64
Sanda Island, 91, 92
Sanda Sound, 90-91
Sandbank, 45
Scalasaig, 129-130
Scalpsie Bay, 66
Scottish Tourist Board, 2
services, 149
Sgat Mor, 68
Shepherd's Point, 46
Silvers' Marine, 52
Skate Island, 68
Skelmorlie Channel, 34
slipway, 2
Sound of Gigha, 92-96
Sound of Islay, 119-127
Sound of Jura, 131-144
Strachur, 80
Stranraer Harbour, 15
Strone, 45
Stroul Bay, 52
Stroul Yacht Haven, 52
submarines, 3
supplies, 149
Swine's Hole, 47

Tarbert, Loch Fyne, 69-72
Tarbert, West Loch, 99-101
Tarbert, Jura, 134
Tarbert, Loch, Jura, 123-127
Taynish Island, 139

Tayvallich, 139, 140
telephone boxes, 6
Texa, 110
tides, 3, 7
Tighnabruaich, 65
Tiree, 130
Tomont End, 39
Torrisdale Bay, 86-87
trailed boats, launching, 2
transport, public, 2
Troon, 21, 23-26

weather forecasts, 3
Wemyss Bay Pier, 39
West Highland Anchorages and Moorings Association (WHAM), 5
West Kyle, 65-67
West Loch Tarbert, 99-101
Whitefarland Bay, 122
Whiting Bay, 31
Wreck Bay, 62

Yachtsman's Almanac, 8